MW00658530

HEALING THE HEART & SOUL

A Five-Step, Soul-Level Healing Process for Transforming Your Life

MICHAEL MIRDAD

GRAIL
PRESS

HEALING THE HEART & SOUL

A Five-Step, Soul-Level Healing Process
for Transforming Your Life

Copyright © 2012 Michael Mirdad
All rights reserved. No part of this publication may be reproduced
or distributed in any form or by any means without the prior written
consent of the author.

GRAIL
PRESS

PO Box 2783
Bellingham, WA 98227
(360) 671-8349
www.GrailProductions.com

Book cover and interior design by
Robert Lanphear
www.lanpheardesign.com

Library of Congress Cataloging-in-Publication Data
Mirdad, Michael.
Healing the Heart & Soul/ Michael Mirdad.
Library of Congress Control Number: 2011929210
ISBN 9780974021669

Second Printing

CONTENTS

ACKNOWLEDGMENTS

This book would not have been possible were it not for the many thousands of clients and friends who applied its principles. These friends/clients are living proof that the concepts and processes found in this book do indeed bring about profound (miraculous) changes and healings in the heart and soul. Many thanks to you all!

My heartfelt thanks go to Lynn, Sally, Jackie, Angela, Judy, David, and Gregg for their diligent proofreading and invaluable feedback. Also thanks to Robin Rose for her artistic input. Thanks once again to Bob Lanphear for his outstanding book design.

As always, I also Give Thanks to God—the Spirit of Love—for providing continued healing and inspiration to me and for guiding me to heal and inspire others.

Lastly, many thanks to you, the reader, who remains committed to your healing and growth. I know that many of you have seen and walked many paths of healing and have not always experienced success. I am grateful that you have not given up your search and have chosen to include my work and/or this book as one of your guides to healing. My prayer is that you are rewarded for your continued faith and trust. I am confident that if you keep an open mind, this material will, in some way, make a difference in your life.

TERMINOLOGY

First, please note that, to make the material in this book as clear as possible, words have been capitalized that ordinarily might not be. For example, the words for each of the five steps of the Soul-Level Healing Process have been capitalized, as well as the words from the five stages of the Soul Transformation Process discussed in my previous book *You're Not Going Crazy . . . You're Just Waking Up!*. Second, although many traditions use the word "mind" to represent our higher nature, this word is too easily confused with the intellectual mind ("lower mind"), rather than the intuitive, imaginative, and creative mind ("higher mind"). So in this book the word "soul," instead of "mind," is often used, since it is far more clear and accurate: the soul and the "higher mind" are synonymous and are both located in the heart center. It is the soul that represents the "chooser" of our reality.

DISCLAIMER

The results of the Soul-Level Healing Process may vary from person to person. Although, as a result of the Soul-Level Healing Process described in this book, several individuals claim to have had some form of "miraculous healing" of a physical or emotional nature, this claim is their interpretation of their experiences. The focus and claims in this book are in relation to the soul and are not focused on healing the denser physical or emotional levels. Lastly, although Soul-Level Healing does indeed often shift or heal the core issues and patterns found within one's soul; until healing is complete, symptoms of the previous core issues may still manifest in a denser (physical or emotional) form.

PREFACE

The book you hold in your hands contains an invaluable secret—a process that leads to deeper healing than most people have ever experienced or dreamed possible. Here, the word "healing" refers to any form of a deep, personal transformation (miracle)—not just physical healing.

The healing technique shared in this book is so successful that it has inspired many authors and various clients to refer to *me* as an "effective healer" or "miracle worker," when in fact it is really the Love and Power of God working through this method that makes it so powerful. Credit also needs to be shared with the numerous other *external* healing modalities used to support this *internal* healing process.

During my 30 years as a spiritual teacher, healer, and counselor, I have seen several thousand clients throughout most states and many countries. During this time, I have worked with issues ranging from minor aches to severe health conditions and from mild forms of depression or sadness to extreme cases of physical or sexual abuse, as well as working with clients who were struggling with relationship and/or prosperity issues.

The Soul-Level Healing Process has proven effective for shifting these and many other issues. The material in this book is a distillation from those many years of experience, as I have done my best to share only the bare essentials needed to effectively and efficiently accomplish internal healing—healing of the heart and soul.

During my many years of sharing healing and counseling work, numerous people have requested that I write a book about the techniques of healing I have developed and practice in my private sessions. People were excited to know why these techniques are so quick and effective in bringing about miraculous shifts, or healings. **This book reveals the necessary ingredients for creating a personal healing at the deepest level—Soul-Level Healing.** It features specific techniques to evoke healing *for* you OR to be used *by* you to bring healing into the lives of your loved ones and/or clients.

Healing the Heart & Soul begins by offering some essential concepts behind healing, as well as providing a deeper understanding as to why some people don't seem to heal. It also covers the roles of forgiveness, mirroring, and miracles in the Soul-Level Healing Process. Then it shares the specific technique of the five-step, Soul-Level Healing Process that will, in nearly every case, uncover the "real" cause (or causes) hidden behind any particular challenge or problem—physical, emotional, mental, financial—even within relationships.

This book has been kept to a manageable size so that the content remains as clear and direct as possible, in order to eliminate possible confusion and not to waste more time between now and your awakening. This book prepares you to heal at deeper levels than ever before. It also prepares you to experience a life of greater inspiration, safety, guidance, and fulfillment.

> *Your function on earth is healing.*
> **–ACIM** (Text 12, VII, 4)

PART ONE

Soul-Level Healing:
The Concept

Chapter 1

INTRODUCTION TO SOUL-LEVEL HEALING

Soul-Level Healing can be defined as "a two-part process of Emptying one's cup of faulty belief systems AND Refilling this cup with new, healthy, and loving systems of belief." In this book, these two parts of the healing process (Emptying and Refilling) are divided (for greater clarity and easier practice) into a five-step process. The five steps for accomplishing a Soul-Level Healing are as follows:

1. Recognize
2. Accept
3. Surrender
4. Refill
5. Give Thanks

The first three steps focus on the *Emptying* of one's cup, while the last two steps focus on the *Refilling* of the cup. Combined, these five steps are, in effect, synonymous with experiencing a miracle or even being "born again."

But now we are . . . dead to that which held us captive, so that we are slaves not under the old written code but in the new life of the Spirit.

–The Bible, Romans 7:6

Ultimately, we are all made in the perfect image of Love and Light—God—and can never really be sick, addicted, or ailing in any way, including financially. Nevertheless, such situations seem to plague humanity on a daily basis. How can this be? How can we have problems when they are, in truth, impossible? The answer is simple: **We have problems because we fail to see clearly enough to experience the true life of Love, Peace, Joy, and Abundance that awaits us on the other side of the veils of our limiting belief systems.** It's not unlike finding ourselves struggling to make our way through a dark room, when turning on a light makes it far easier to see where we are going. To better understand the concept of Soul-Level Healing, the metaphor of turning on the light is akin to experiencing a true healing or a miracle. Such incredible shifts merely illuminate our minds so we can see what was there all along—Heaven.

Heaven is all around you but you have to lift the veils to see it.

–Buddha

We, as human beings, have five primary aspects, symbolized in our five limbs and the five fingers and toes on each hand and foot respectively. The lower four aspects (symbolizing our humanness) are represented in the four lower chakras (energy centers) found in the body's torso. The fifth aspect (a collection of the three chakras found in the head and neck symbolizing our divinity) is really one—just as the trinity of Spirit is really ONE. These five primary aspects are also symbolic of the five elements— four earthly (earth, water, fire and air) and one spiritual (ether). Our fifth aspect, Spirit, is always Holy and perfect, although we can seem to suffer dis-ease or some other form of disconnection on one of the other four levels (physical/energetic, emotional, mental, and heart/soul). In fact, the more we feel disconnected from our higher self, the more our lives (health, relationships, finances, etc.) suffer. **Healing of the soul, therefore, is crucial for reconnecting with the higher self to end suffering.**

Again, although healing might be needed on any of the four human levels, it is not needed on the level of Spirit, where all is well. In fact, it is the "drawing down" of Love and Light *from* this fifth level/element of Spirit that brings about the final step in Soul-Level Healing. **Although we may have some disease in the body, emotions, and/or the mind, all disorder originates from the diseased (and false) belief systems held**

in the heart and soul. Once these diseased belief systems (issues and patterns) are seen and released, they need to be replaced with new and higher level belief systems—those that come pouring in from Heaven above—from the Spirit that resides in the highest aspect of our being. Otherwise, healing will be limited, delayed, or not seen at all.

Any healing that falls short of healing the soul, falls short of true healing and merely creates a smokescreen like a "sleight of hand," or temporary manipulation of appearances within the material world. The five steps of Soul-Level Healing, on the other hand, create a complete process for the potential healing of any issue of the mind, body, soul, and even life's circumstances. **The various other modalities of healing the body, energy-systems, emotions, and mind are still valuable because they bring hope and at least some relief to those who would otherwise continue to suffer.**

Since Soul-Level Healing utilizes (and/or endorses) all other modalities of healing as a means of supporting the healing within the soul, it is easy to blend or reconcile the steps of the Soul-Level Healing Process with any other system or philosophy of healing, thereby increasing the potential in other systems for a healing of the soul.

Healing, consequently, can be assisted through many different modalities, which include the following:

Physical-Level Healing—medicine, herbs, nutrition, yoga, tai chi, surgery, acupuncture, aromatherapy, chi kung, massage, and all forms of body work, as well as all forms of energy healing, such as reiki

Emotional-Level Healing—inner child work, counseling, recovery work, sexual abuse therapy, family of origin healing, co-dependence healing, and breath-work

Mental-Level Healing—hypnotherapy, neuro-linguistic-programming, EFT (Emotional Freedom Technique), reconnective healing, and all healing modalities that primarily work through the nervous system

Remember, **Spirit created us as a perfect reflection of Its Love and Light. Therefore, the need for miracles exists within humankind and not within God.** The problems (large or small) that seem to plague humankind begin in our hearts, minds, and souls and then manifest, or become apparent, in our physical world and in our lives. So, although there appears to be a problem on the material level, it began somewhere in between the perfect realm of Spirit and the less than perfect realm of matter. The problem began in the realm of the soul, where we hold our mistaken core beliefs, and it is only in the realm of the soul that the problem can ultimately be healed.

We certainly can manifest small shifts in all areas of living by using technology, force, medicine, and other forms of self-will. However, since a *true* miracle, or shift, must first reach the higher mind or soul (which is beyond human technology), man-made shifts are merely temporary fixes—not miracles. A true miracle, on the other hand, involves a Soul-Level Healing—resulting in unlimited or expansive versions of feeling "born again." **Though you *can't* go back and create a new beginning, you *can* begin now and create a new ending.**

He left yesterday behind him, you might say
he's "born again," you might say he found the
key for every door . . . Talk to God and listen
to the casual reply . . . Rocky Mountain High . . .
–John Denver
(Song:"Rocky Mountain High")

Soul-Level Healing typically involves going through some form of the following five steps:

1. **Recognizing** the need for healing is the point wherein a person chooses to make a significant change for the better in his or her life. The person has somehow come to Recognize that his or her life, as it is, is not going well and therefore is in need of a change, healing, miracle, or transformation. This Step of Rec-

ognizing takes courage because most people would prefer not to admit that they have a problem, as this would mean that they then have to deal with it. But once most people finally acknowledge there is a problem, they usually make the effort to seek out a form of healing or healers that can work with them to make the necessary changes in their lives.

2. **Accepting** the deeper causes of our Recognized issues is usually the most powerful or cathartic of the five steps, but this can vary with each person and scenario. Accepting does not mean simply acquiescing to the problem. Instead, Accepting entails becoming empowered and taking responsibility for tracking down the deeper causes of the problem— which can be accomplished through the "tracking exercise" taught in this book.

   Before proceeding to the third step of Surrender, it's important to mention that the length of time for using this five-step process varies and can manifest in a "short," "medium," or "long" form. (See Worksheets #1, #2, and #3 at the back of the book for a detailed description of the Soul-Level Healing Process in all three forms.) Although the *short* form lasts less than a minute, it can be completely effective in transforming whatever physical (health, financial, etc.) or emotional (relationships, sadness, etc.) issue is being brought up for healing. The *medium* form usually takes five to ten minutes. The *long* form usually takes between ten to thirty minutes or more.

One of the differences between the three lengths of time used in the healing process is found in the Accepting step. This difference manifests in the following manner: (1) In the *short* form of the Accepting Step, you simply acknowledge that there are, indeed, some known or unknown wounds that have remained unhealed and are now causing your symptom or problem. These wounds are then Surrendered and Refilled with heightened states of consciousness. (2) In the *medium* form of the Accepting Step, however, instead of simply acknowledging the fact that there is "something" beneath the surface causing your problem, you go a step further and spend some time tracking down these unhealed wounds, so that they may be uprooted more effectively. During such tracking (which can be done *on* yourself or *for* others), you gain greater insights into *who* and/or *what* (event) rooted the old wounds into your soul. (3) During the *long* form of the Accepting Step, you may also verbally and physically express some of the pent-up emotions that are locked into the body and/or soul. This releasing occurs in a safe environment and involves the use of some healthy, cathartic process—such as anger release—OR perhaps a ceremony ("cord cutting," for example) to bring closure to an old, traumatic experience.

To summarize, with each of the three differing lengths of the healing process explained above, there is progressively more investigation into the hidden causes of the current issue AND often proportionately a greater amount of cathartic release—although not always.

3. **Surrendering** of everything that surfaces during the Accepting step or tracking exercise can take one or more of several forms. Surrender can include prayerfully giving some problem or issue to God; crying it away; releasing through deep sighing breaths; setting an intention to release; journaling or writing a goodbye note, then burning it, and seeing it dissipate as smoke into the ether. Whatever the choice, you are Surrendering to Spirit the issue you brought in for healing and whatever came up in the tracking portion of the exercise. This Surrendering includes memories of, and grievances concerning, all people (including yourself), events, emotions, and whatever else came up during your tracking. You are Surrendering *everything* as thoroughly and unconditionally as possible, thus making room to be

Refilled with the Loving Presence of God—which occurs in the next step.

The Soul-Level Healing Process is not unlike gardening, with the Surrender Step being the time you spend throwing away the rocks and weeds you dug up (during the Acceptance Step) to make room for the seeds of a new life.

4. **Refilling** is the process that naturally follows the emptying of oneself that occurs during the steps of Recognizing, Accepting, and Surrendering. Although it may seem obvious to Refill with something healthy and new, after an Emptying of the old, Refilling is the most neglected, overlooked step of any healing—especially most forms of emotional healing.

Most healers and counselors know how to Recognize the external problems (or symptoms) of their clients. However, many counselors and healers fall short and fail to take their clients any further than the steps of Accepting or Surrendering, and for good reasons. First of all, they are not trained to go further. Second, to truly accomplish the Refilling Step, facilitators would have to incorporate some form of spirituality into their work—which is usually not only lacking but, in fact, is discouraged within most of the health and counseling professions.

A few healers and counselors may encourage *some*

simple form of Refilling, such as taking a few centering breaths or thinking a positive thought or perhaps stating a personal affirmation. However, all of these pale in comparison to the act of consciously calling in the healing Presence of God and doing so in a vivid, tangible manner. Therefore it is always advisable to seek out healers and counselors who know how to reach this Step of Refilling. These might include some of the healers who do such work as "soul-retrieval" or some *advanced* forms of "hypnotherapy."

Re-filling is an immeasurably vital step in the Soul-Level Healing Process, as it allows us to reprogram ourselves with new patterns, altering the blueprint (or matrix) of our consciousness, which is what eventually manifests as the outer projection we call life.

5. **Giving Thanks** is probably the most effective method of bringing closure to the past, whether that past is hurtful or happy. Giving Thanks also allows the universe to hear a statement from you that says, "Yes, thank you! I received my lessons or gifts (things that have already materialized *or* things you just finished praying for but have not yet seen), and I am ready to move on to the next level."

Giving Thanks also demonstrates a humble heart and an "attitude of gratitude." Such humility and appreciation attracts the loving support of angels and all other loving intelligence in the universe. Furthermore, to Give Thanks means that you, the human soul, are acknowledging that there is a Creative Spirit that is greater than the part of you that is suffering. This Divine Presence, therefore, remembers your divine nature. It is to this Divine Spirit that you are Giving Thanks.

Chapter 2

CORE ISSUES
AND CORE PATTERNS

The word "core" is synonymous with "heart" or "center." Therefore, it is accurate to say that healing the heart and soul is the same as healing one's core issues. For healing to be complete, it has to reach and include the core, or heart and soul. And when we access the heart and soul, we are sure to find the core programs that create and control our lives. The core programs of our souls contain primarily three types of "files": (1) our core beliefs; (2) our core issues; and (3) our core patterns. Each of these core programs, individually or in any combination, make up every aspect of the daily manifestations of what we call life—from health and relationships to finances and careers.

To get at the core of God at his greatest, one must first get into the core of himself at his least.

–Meister Eckhart

Just as we humans have a *physical* "core" that we strengthen to improve health and physical fitness, we also have a personal, *spiritual* core. **Our spiritual cores are strengthened not through physical exercise, but through such spiritual practices as concentration and meditation exercises, as well as by upholding (or maintaining) healthy, personal boundaries.** Our spiritual cores are also heavily influenced (positively or negatively) by the core beliefs, core issues, and core patterns held within our hearts and souls, which figuratively impact us from two directions: (1) downloaded from "above"—our various core programs including the core belief that we are separate from Spirit or God; and (2) uploaded from "below"—our accumulated issues and patterns from life's experiences.

> *You see what you expect, and you*
> *expect what you invite.*
> –**ACIM** (Text 12, VII, 5)

The core issues and patterns relating to our connection to Spirit are determined by *one* major belief: how much we believe we are separate from God (and from each other). Most of us would never consciously think that we hold such a belief. But that's just the problem—this isn't a conscious thought. The belief that we are separate from God is even deeper than the subconscious mind. This belief is held deep in the recesses of the soul. **The core *belief* that we are separate from God gives birth to a couple of core *issues* (such as feelings of emptiness, low self-worth, or feeling unlovable). These then create our core *patterns* (such as being betrayed, being alone, or experiencing lack) that ultimately make up the structure of our lives.** For example, if you *believe* you are separate from God, this false belief might then give birth to a core *issue* that you are unlovable. This core *issue* then might manifest as a core *pattern* of being betrayed or abandoned by people you care about and might also then manifest in various unhealthy ways, such as your partner cheating on you.

> *It does not matter if you think you are in earth or Heaven. What . . . [God] wills of you can never change. The truth in you remains as radiant as a star, as pure as light, as innocent as love itself.*
> –ACIM (Text 31, VI, 7)

As already mentioned, core issues and core patterns not only *descend* from above (from the beliefs held in the soul), but they also *ascend* from below (from the wounds of daily life). The good news, however, is that although our many ongoing unhealthy beliefs, issues, and patterns set up a life of limitation and woundedness; forgiveness and love are all we need to release these layers—thus making room for the new, healthy programs and patterns of A New Life.

Generally speaking, there are two primary methods for healing our core beliefs, issues, and patterns found within the soul. The first method, and the approach in this book, is through the five-step, Soul-Level Healing Process. The second is a process referred to as "Dismantling." The former of these two methods involves emptying the old mental "programs" of past wounds, issues, patterns, and so forth, and replacing them with new programs of Love, Peace, Joy, and Abundance.

The latter of these two methods—Dismantling—involves a procedure that is not unlike that recommended by Buddha, which is to use your "rational mind" to break down or disassemble your problems. This procedure allows you to take issues that would otherwise seem overwhelming and out of your control and reduce them to manageable challenges. Dismantling is commonly used for such emergencies as panic attacks or any seemingly unsolvable crisis—mild or major. Choosing to Dismantle any issue you can't seem to heal is always a wise decision, because whatever issues you fail to Dismantle in your life, usually turn and Dismantle you.

Another reason for choosing this latter method (Dismantling) might be that you don't seem to have time to do more extensive healing or perhaps it seems as though the five-step process isn't working. Or you might, for example, feel anxious over the outcome of a medical test or a court case. In such a situation, instead of doing the Soul-Level Healing Process, you could ask yourself some rational questions designed to Dismantle the concern and anxiety around the situation: "What is really going on here?" "What is the worst case scenario?" Asking such questions often assists in recognizing that things are not as bad as you might have thought and/or that rarely do things go as poorly as you might have feared.

Chapter 3

HEALING
AND MIRACLES

The word "healing" can easily be replaced by the words "restoration" or "miracle," as they all indicate a shift and because one does not occur without the other. A true *miracle* (most commonly an *internal* experience) is defined *not* by the manifestation of some external phenomenon (like levitation) but rather is defined by the *healing* of the soul's (or mind's) belief systems. More specifically, it could be said that a significant shift (for the better) in a person's belief system will bring about a miracle, or restoration, to the person's soul or life.

To experience a true healing (shift of consciousness at the level of the heart and soul), therefore, requires recognizing that an *internal* miracle is different from an *external* miracle. *An internal* miracle is far more "real" (lasting) and synonymous with healing. On the surface, this may not seem so. If, for example, we take an aspirin and it deadens the pain of a headache, we might mistake the lessening of pain for an actual "healing." This *external* healing, although valuable to our physical comfort, is clearly not the same as experiencing a miracle (a complete shift in consciousness). With this in mind, we are left with the conclusion that **true healing is miraculous, and it is *miraculous* to experience true healing.**

The Divinely inspired book called "*A Course in Miracles*" refers to this miraculous healing process as a shift in perception or consciousness—meaning a shift at the deepest level of the soul. When such healing occurs through powerful healing processes, the effects can, and will, flow down the manifestation ladder until they are perceivable in the outer world. In other words, **true healing and miracles (shifts in perception) must take place in the heart and soul before actually reaching the body.** This understanding reveals a deeper reason why some of our "healings" do not last. **We may have experienced a shift in the body or even an emotional release, but the healing is not real or permanent unless we have healed at the heart and soul level—the source of the problem.**

Miracles (or healings) can be experienced *internally* or *externally*. *Internal* healing is the greater of the two, because an *internal* miracle has the power to trigger an *external* miracle, but the opposite is not always the case.

An *internal* miracle usually occurs within the higher mind (heart and soul) and can then interrupt, or intercede into, what is believed to be a "natural and usually harmful or limiting course of events," triggering an *external* miracle. The *external* miracle, resulting from an internal shift, can loosely be described as having three stages: (1) We seem to have a crisis or problem. (2) A shift occurs that alters the course that would otherwise have resulted in a greater crisis. (3) We have a different outcome from what was expected, thanks to our miracle.

There are generally two groups of clients looking for healing: The first group includes those who want to heal physically and/or emotionally but want to avoid dealing with the Soul-Level issues behind their illness. Of course if they receive such healing, it would reinforce their ego-beliefs that the body (and its condition) is who they really are and the body is the main focus for healing. The reinforcement of these false beliefs would then seem to give the body the power to make itself sick or healthy. The second group seeking healing, on the other hand, includes those who know that the human body and its conditions of sickness or health are merely thoughts in the mind. Therefore, such people place little or no emphasis on the condition of the body, since they understand that the mind or soul is all that really matters, as it is their *true* identity. People in the latter group have their mental (belief) priorities straight, and seem to be the ones who most often heal and recover in body and soul.

Typically when we pray for a miracle, we are asking for relief from the *external*, manifested symptoms of problems that, again, began in our souls. Therefore, *external* miracles appear to be limited and never predictable as to the timing or form of their manifestation. In other words, since we pray for quick fixes or limited answers, the resulting external miracles, or shifts, are vague—sometimes seen and often not. Conversely, if our minds remain open and non-limiting as to what form our miracles take, we then can experience the greatest miracles possible. Therefore, **when we pray for a miracle, we should be praying for a *feeling*, or shift in *awareness* (*internal* miracle), and not a *thing* (*external* miracle).** Soul-Level Healing coincides with an *internal*, miraculous shift in the soul that then can manifest *externally* in the life of the recipient.

> *The prayer of heart does not really ask*
> *for concrete things. It always requests*
> *some kind of* [internal] *experience.*
> **–ACIM** (Manual 21, 2)

The various means for manifesting a miracle (internally *or* externally) are countless. Prayer is the means we are most familiar with for opening to, or requesting, a miracle. But advanced healing techniques are also among the most likely means of creating a miracle, for they are much like a practical form of prayer. Remember, a prayer is a call for a miracle, or a healing, or a shift from fear to safety, hate to love, poverty to prosperity, or sickness to health. Therefore, **a healing technique that facilitates such a shift, or transformation, is a practical method for manifesting a miracle**.

Furthermore, the manifestation of miracles can be viewed as a restoration of Divine Order. For example, in a healthy person, the energy and experience of the soul is one of flow, rhythm, life, love, and trust. In an unhealthy person, or anyone who is in an unhealthy (traumatic) environment, the flow stops; the rhythm becomes erratic; life and love become frozen, and trust becomes limited and conditional. This is not the way our lives were meant to be. Yes, we have free will, but healing occurs when we use our will to choose Divine Order over chaos. This *restoration* to the Peace and Love of Divine Order *is* a "miracle."

There are at least two ways of accessing and triggering a miracle in the form of a healing (or Soul-Level Healing). One way is to directly connect with the soul and its core memory (akashic record) and then proceed with an effective form of healing. However, since such a technique is not understood or familiar to everyone, there is another option accessible to all. This other method is that of holistic healing.

The field of holistic healing (like all other arts and sciences) is currently making a quantum leap forward. Now, more than ever, humanity is gaining a deeper perspective into the connection between spirituality and healing. Science, for example, is gaining a new respect for the delicate and intricate relationship between body, emotions, mind, and soul (heart).

The term "holistic" (whole-istic) as it relates to healing is the same as the term "holographic" (whole-o-graphic) as it relates to quantum science. Both fields, holistic healing and quantum science, are exploring the theory that all things are interconnected—that the *whole* also can be accessed through any *part*. With this in mind, **the heart and soul can be accessed through their microcosmic representation in any other part of our being.** Therefore, some level of the heart and soul can be accessed through any supportive healing method *if* the healer and client are open to utilizing the healing method *holistically*. However, the healer needs to see the technique as a *means* to accessing the soul-level issue generated by trauma, rather than as an *end* in itself.

Since a trauma can be stored at such diverse levels of consciousness as the physical body, the energy body, or the emotional body, working with these various bodies can be a means for triggering a healing deep enough to reach the heart and soul. As healers access their higher senses and clients develop a deeper commitment to healing, techniques that more accurately find and efficiently release such energy blocks will be created and utilized more frequently. This advancement will then give birth to new opportunities for healing in all parts of our lives and being.

Again, although the *soul* (or mind) *can* make a person sick and create challenges in his or her life, the *body cannot* make the soul sick per se. What the body can do is send the soul fearful images and events—tempting the soul to choose to believe in them. Then, once these painful or fearful events are anchored into the soul (or mind) and thus become negative beliefs, these negative images and events become imbued with creative powers to then affect a person's core issues, patterns, and experiences.

The above views on healing seem to leave us with a paradox: If the only form of true healing takes place *internally* (in the soul), then why bother with any of the numerous forms of *external* healing? The answer is that even though the body *cannot* heal the soul, healing the body *can* help to trigger a healing *in* the soul. For example, **if the healer and/or modality are holistic** and effective enough, whatever healing work performed should in some manner direct the recipient within and toward the core of the real issue—the wounds of the soul. This, in effect, allows the *external* healing technique to have an *internal* affect. Since the healing technique also addressed some external symptoms, it might prove to create more relief than if the healing had only been addressed internally. For example, if a river is slightly blocked, an increase in the water flow up-stream (soul) will eventually wash the block away. Yet also dealing with the block of debris at its own level (body) will increase the chances of the stream unblocking sooner.

> *The value of . . .* [healing] *does not lie in the manner in which it is expressed. In fact, if it is used truly, it will inevitably be expressed in whatever way is most helpful to the receiver. This means that a miracle, to attain its full efficacy, must be expressed in a language that the recipient can understand . . . This does not necessarily mean that this is the highest level of . . .* [healing] *of which he* [or she] *is capable. It does mean, however, that it is the highest level of communication of which he is capable now.*
> **–ACIM** (Text 2, IV, 5)

Thus, the various healers and healing arts are invaluable to us as support systems to the Soul-Level Healing Process. The various modalities of herbs, aromas, bodywork, counseling, energy-work, and so forth can act as access points and triggers for Soul-Level Healing. In the end, **Soul-Level Healing is a necessity, while any other form of healing is merely a wise addition.**

Chapter 4

FORGIVENESS

As previously mentioned, the words "healing" and "miracles" can be viewed as nearly synonymous—the only difference being that it takes one to activate the other. "Healing" and "miracles" can also be viewed as synonymous with the word "forgiveness," especially since forgiveness is the most powerful means of creating a healing or miracle.

Forgiveness literally transforms vision, and lets you see the real world reaching quietly and gently across chaos, removing all illusions.

–ACIM (Text 17, II)

"Forgiveness" is possibly one of the most misunderstood and misused words and concepts in the worlds of religion and spirituality. **The act of forgiveness should actually be called the "Art of Forgiveness." As is true with the development of any skill, it takes practice, determination, tenacity, and willingness to create things anew.**

Forgiveness can enter our lives the easy way (by recognizing its value and choosing it) or the hard way (by becoming tired of feeling the painful effects of non-forgiveness, or false forgiveness, and being forced to experience the humbling process of "Dismantling"). In either case, true forgiveness requires that we be open to seeing people and events differently. We also have to demonstrate a willingness to relinquish our hurts and anger (judgments) concerning all relevant people and events. Additionally, we are called to take responsibility for any part we may have played in creating discordant or hurtful events. **When we learn to take responsibility for our own lives, we soon find that we no longer place inappropriate expectations or projections onto others.** This huge step (of taking responsibility for our pain) is the most difficult, since most people don't know how to track down the part they may have played in creating discordant situations, not to mention that they usually don't want to. But, ignorance is not an escape from the law of responsibility.

Although one may assume that the act of forgiveness is always sincere, this is unfortunately *not* always the case. There are many forms of "false forgiveness." **False forgiveness includes forgiving out of pity or obligation or making deals or pretending that time has healed us.** Or, we may think we have forgiven when, in actuality, we have learned to deny that we are hurt or make excuses for those who we think have hurt us.

False forgiveness is usually founded on keeping someone in the assigned role of "victim," which automatically suspends any chance to experience healing and forgiveness. The more dramatized these roles (victim/victimizer) become, the more entrenched the hurt will be, thus rendering forgiveness even more difficult. There is no escaping the fact that we cannot experience true forgiveness while hiding, denying, defending or protecting our hurts. However, a healthy and true forgiveness process, such as Soul-Level Healing, offers a solution for this dilemma of pain and denial.

Whatever *modus operandi* for "escaping" *true* forgiveness we may practice (and no matter how entrenched this defense may be), there are ways out of this self-imposed prison. For some people, it helps to chip away at their wounds a little at a time by talking about their hurts to someone they can trust. For other people, it might help to write a letter to the person they perceive as having hurt them. This letter should express as many of their hurt feelings as possible and as honestly as possible. It's best to allow this letter-writing process to be a deeply emotional experience. When the letter is complete, it should be burned—not mailed—while saying a prayer and asking that these hurts be dissolved and their weight lifted. Others might prefer a more dramatic and cathartic approach to breaking open their trapped wounds. Such approaches could involve healing workshops, anger release work, or even going on retreat to a healing sanctuary or a pilgrimage to a holy site wherein the pains could be "prayed over" and left behind. Whatever your choice, **there must be some degree of allowing your cup (soul) to be emptied, thus making room for it to be Refilled by God.** And it is truly impossible to say which is the more profound in its effects towards healing: Emptying out the old (as in forgiveness) or Refilling with the new (as in seeing the presence of Spirit in self and others), since they are merely two sides of the same coin—healing.

Besides the numerous forms of "false forgiveness," there also are many versions, or levels, of well-intended forgiveness that follow a natural progression from the least to the most advanced form of forgiveness. Even the most basic of these forms is valuable because, after all, *any* attempt to forgive is better than no attempt of any kind. What matters most is that we personally evolve enough to apply the highest form of which we feel capable—while developing deeper and deeper levels of forgiveness—eventually applied toward all people and events. These various forms of forgiveness are as follows:

1. **Fundamental Forgiveness:** Even those who doubt the existence of God can muster up the attempt to "forgive" or "overlook" the "wrong-doing" of another. However, choosing to overlook the deeds of others does not mean we have actually forgiven them.

2. **Religious Forgiveness:** Religions usually teach that we can call on God to assist us in forgiving. This is done by asking God to forgive our errors and to assist us in forgiving the errors of others. Although definitely a move in the right direction, we eventually learn to play an even more responsible role in the choice to forgive.

3. **Intellectual Forgiveness:** We think "time heals all wounds" and that just because time has gone by and our wounds seem to hurt less, we have "forgiven" those who wronged us. Yes, we may indeed feel better as time passes, but time itself is an illusion and possesses no power to heal either us or our wounds. At some point we will be called back to the job of forgiving that which we had previously placed on "pause."

4. **Compassionate Forgiveness:** Here we learn to forgive others by choosing to see the person who has "wronged" us as wounded and worthy of our love and forgiveness. This is an empowering concept, as it encourages us to develop a compassionate heart.

This form of forgiveness falls short, however, if it encourages people to justify another person's negative circumstances in order to generate the pity and compassion necessary to forgive them. Ultimately, we need to progress to forgiving others even when they don't have a "hard-luck" story. Instead, we forgive no matter who they are, where they have been, or what they have done.

5. **Spiritual Forgiveness:** Spiritual forgiveness is a sincere attempt to practice forgiving the way God forgives. Since God always remains in Its purest Mind, It can only see purity, rather than flaws, and therefore sees nothing to forgive. At this level, the highest of human understanding, we realize that ultimately there is no-body and no-thing to forgive—neither in ourselves nor in others. Here we understand that if ever anyone truly *did* harm us, that person merely acted out some unhealed issue we once held inside of ourselves. We now realize that to truly experience forgiveness for others, we must also forgive (heal) the core issues within ourselves.

If you fail to completely forgive someone or something, you cannot completely heal. It's that simple! All excuses for having not forgiven are subtle forms of unconsciously *choosing* to hold onto your judgments and the resulting pain you will then inflict on yourself and others. "You can run but you can't hide." **Keep an honest eye on how you may claim you have forgiven something only to bring it up again and again, which is clear proof that all judgment has not yet been released.** No matter how clever you (and your ego) may be, if you still have any judgments in your consciousness, they will inevitably surface and be seen, spoken, felt, and/or experienced in your outer life—especially in your relations and interactions with others.

Those that find fault with others will find fault in themselves; for they are writing their own record—they must meet, every one, that which they have said about another; for so is the image, the soul of the Creator in each body, and when ye speak evil of or unkindly to thy brother, thou hast done it unto thy God.

–Edgar Cayce

Whether the decision is made consciously or unconsciously, **when you choose not to forgive a person or an event that seems to have harmed you, it also means you are then, by default, choosing to be in pain—physically, emotionally, mentally, and/or in your life's circumstances.** Furthermore, you will feel guilty for holding this resentment, and this feeling of guilt will cause even greater pain in your heart and soul. Guilt acts like an infection that has taken root in your wound and thus prevents you from healing.

Spiritual forgiveness heals you of the perception of being separate from God, which in turn accomplishes a mini-version of your return Home. If it is true that your ego has no intention of letting you off the hook easily, it certainly will keep trying to prevent you from healing and forgiving. Whether consciously or subconsciously, the ego encourages a constant state of fear and resistance that screams, "Make them (people in the present) suffer for how I feel and for what was done to me (usually in the past)." But forgiveness sings, "Let it go!" Or, as *A Course in Miracles* puts it, say to those who have hurt you, "God is the love with which I forgive you."

> *We win by tenderness;*
> *we conquer by forgiveness.*
>
> **–F. W. Robertson**

Of course it seems easier to forgive those whom you have deemed "deserving" of your forgiveness or whom you have had the time to gradually choose to forgive. However the **real work of forgiveness comes from those people who catch you off guard when you're not in the "mood" to forgive.** These are the best people with which to practice healing. These are the folks who offer you an opportunity for your greatest advancements. Learn to laugh at the fact that you were caught unprepared and attempting to ignore a potential for forgiveness—but don't forget to forgive. At first it may not be easy to see such situations as opportunities for spiritual advancement, but eventually you will begin to see the rewards of peace and joy that come from choosing to forgive everyone at all times. **When you truly forgive, you are coming closer to "being as God" than in any other moment, because to truly forgive means to see and feel only the light within yourself and others, as God sees.**

"A monk was sitting by the edge of a river when all of a sudden he saw a scorpion falling into the water. The monk reached out to save the scorpion, only to be stung by it. The scorpion fell again into the water and the monk reached out for the second time, only to be stung by the scorpion again. Once again the scorpion fell into the water, and as the monk reached out to save him, an observer asked the monk; 'Excuse me, but why do you keep reaching out to such an ungrateful creature when all it does is sting you every time you save it?' The monk replied, 'Because the nature of the scorpion is to sting, but the true nature of the human is to save [love and forgive].'"

–Anonymous

The fear-based ego part of your mind always tries to hide and get rid of your unforgiven (unhealed) traits and experiences by projecting them onto others. What could have been acknowledged and seen as merely temporary errors in need of forgiveness are now perceived as permanent and unforgivable "sins." **Love (God) forgives, but fear (the ego) condemns.** Therefore love or forgiveness can undo whatever the ego tries to accomplish through the memories and emotions of your unhealed fear, hurt, and anger. The ego, on the other hand, needs to feed such negative emotions by keeping alive the "debts" of what it thinks others owe you for hurting you. These perceived debts will keep you from being free to experience the Peace and Love of God. If you are released and forgiven through releasing and forgiving others, then the ego is dissolved and ceases to exist—an ending it fights to prevent.

It may look and feel as though others have *clearly* "caused" your hurts and wounds, but in truth, others are more often merely rubbing up against old wounds that already existed long before you even met the people presently involved. So be courageous enough to let others off the hook for whatever you believe they did to you. Even if others (by human standards) have indeed hurt you, you can still forgive them so that you don't remain with them in a hell of hurt and blame.

*To blame others for your misfortunes, shows
you are in need of education. To blame yourself,
shows your education has begun. To blame no
one, shows your education is complete.*

–Epictetus

Forgiveness may not happen today, but once you
have had enough of the cycle of error, guilt, suffering,
and payback—which usually only results in more error and the continuation of the same cycle—**you will
choose to release all those whom you have imprisoned
for their perceived misdeeds.** But why wait until you
are exhausted from this process of condemning and
pardoning? Choose to release everyone NOW!

*Whenever you stand praying, forgive,
if you have anything against anyone.*
–The Bible, Mark 11:25

Some of us refuse to believe that we hold any judgments and perhaps even claim to feel "only love for
everyone." Of course, if this were true, we would probably have ascended by now. The truth is, **as long as
we notice the difference between the colors of people's
skins or the difference between victims and victimizers,
our souls retain some untrue perceptions that originate**

in unhealed judgments. God holds no such judgments or perceptions of differences.

Ultimately, all that we actually forgive are the illusions, or false perceptions, we once held about others, which are ultimately false perceptions or judgments we held about ourselves. In releasing such perceptions, our souls are restored to their original state of grace. All problems and illnesses are related to wounded perceptions and are healed through the miracle of forgiveness. We are released *as* we release others. This truth is expressed in an ancient prayer stated in a new way: **"Forgiven are our debts, *as* we have forgiven others."**

A Course in Miracles teaches us that all the *external* issues in our lives are really reflections of *internal* issues that need to be Recognized and forgiven. Such internal issues include every type of core issue or core pattern, including fear and low self-esteem.

As already mentioned, at the root of all core issues is the belief that we are separate from God. This erroneous belief usually results in feelings of guilt and/or emptiness. Guilt then births such other emotions as shame, while emptiness births low self-esteem and various forms of addiction (drinking, sex, drugs, co-dependence, etc.).

We first try to deal with all such core issues by *repressing* them. If or when this fails, we *project* the unhealed emotions (often in the form of hurt and anger) into our world and onto other people, much like a film projector sends images onto a motion picture screen. This, of course, by analogy means having to hire some actors to play all the appropriate roles, usually in the form of our many types of relationships (family, friends, partners, children, etc.). The screen, therefore, merely mirrors (or reflects) the stories projected onto it by us, the script writers and directors.

> *The world you see is . . . the outside picture of*
> *an inward condition* [thought or belief system].
>
> **–ACIM** (Text 21, Intro.)

Of course this projection is not a *conscious* process, but we are, nevertheless, bound to the responsibility for seeing and experiencing whatever is projected from our hearts and souls. Therefore, if our hearts are filled with anger, hurt, or pain, we will witness and experience lives that reflect these conditions. But **if our hearts are filled with unconditional love, as well as true, authentic forgiveness for all that once felt unloving, we will just as certainly witness such reflections in our lives—usually in the form of Love, Peace, Joy, and Abundance.**

In the final analysis, since it is your *choice* to release an old hurt, resentment or judgment, which results in forgiveness and healing, it could honestly be said that you heal by *choosing* to forgive those hurts. This, of course, confirms that healing *is* a choice. In other words, **others may have hurt you, but your choice to not forgive kept the pain and suffering alive.** Therefore, your life *cannot* and *will not* improve faster than *you* improve, and **you cannot and will not improve faster than your ability to love and forgive.** Conversely, when you say, "No," to living a life of love and forgiveness, you keep yourself bound to the past and out of the moment—wherein Peace is found. When you say, "Yes," to true forgiveness, you are immediately shifted into a state of "grace"—not the kind of grace where you are granted some sort of spiritual amnesty, but the grace that exists in the mind and soul of one who has accepted his or her original identity—holy and sinless. Remember that **this lifetime has only one purpose, which is for us to heal ourselves and others through the giving and receiving of love, which is best initiated through the act/art of forgiveness.**

> *The greatest thing, you'll ever learn, is just to love, and be loved, in return.*
> **–Nat King Cole** (Song: "Nature Boy")

The following is a sample of true forgiveness as practiced by the ancient Lemurians and later in an ancient

Hawaiian tradition. This forgiveness process is known as *Ho'oponopono*, which means "to make right" the wrongs done in our relations. This incredible process not only offers a simple and effective means of forgiveness but, when understood at a deeply spiritual level, also teaches us, the practitioners, how to take total responsibility for whatever we perceive—even if it involves seeing a sick person. In the mind of the average thinker, what we see outside of ourselves has little or nothing to do with us, which supposedly is proven by the fact that it is "outside" of us. In *Ho'oponopono*, as well as in *A Course in Miracles*, however, the fact that it seems to be outside of us is evidence of how much effort we are willing to use to push away this unwanted issue (our unhealed wounds)—even if it means "dropping" our issue into the life (and onto the shoulders) of someone else. Therefore, a primary reason we end up asking others for forgiveness is that we have done them an injustice when we projected our *own* issues onto them.

The words in this process of asking forgiveness (*Ho'oponopono*) are very simple and only involve repeating a few short sentences, which can be done silently to oneself when addressed to someone who is ailing or not present. Or, they can be spoken aloud when making amends to someone present—provided the person agrees to listen to you do so. The words of

Ho'oponopono are as follows:

I love you.

I'm sorry.

Please forgive me.

Thank you.

A Course in Miracles shares a similar philosophy of healing and could be seen in the context of *Ho'oponopono* as follows:

Ho'oponopono: *I love you.*

ACIM: I love you because of who you really are—God's perfect and holy child—the Christ.

Ho'oponopono: *I'm sorry.*

ACIM: I am sorry for forgetting your true identity and judging you as being capable of being sick (poor, depressed, etc.).

Ho'oponopono: *Please forgive me.*

ACIM: Please forgive me for having projected my unhealed wounds and limiting beliefs onto you, thus co-creating your challenge. I too forgive myself, for I too have suffered by allowing you to bear the cross of my issues.

Ho'oponopono: *Thank you.*

ACIM: Thank you for mirroring to me that which needed to be Recognized, Accepted, Surrendered, and Refilled with the Presence of Truth (the Truth of who we are). As we now stand forgiven (by each other), we also stand healed and one in God, as God. And so it is!

Chapter 5

MIRRORING

Have you ever found yourself expressing a frustration about someone in your life, and a friend exclaims, "Well, that person must be mirroring something about yourself that you don't want to look at!"? Your friend may be well-meaning, but such use of the term and concept "mirroring" is limited and over-simplified.

The concept, or "law," of mirroring basically can be explained as follows: **Because the world (and universe) around us is believed to be a three-dimensional holographic manifestation of the conscious and subconscious thoughts within our minds and souls, it can be said that the universe is indeed reflecting (or mirroring) back to us whatever we are feeling, thinking, and believing consciously and subconsciously.** The concept of mirroring should not be limited or oversimplified.

These reflections are meant to get our attention and to show us something about our inner selves that we are probably ignoring and need to see literally magnified onto the holographic screen of our lives.

You must look in before you look out . . .
As you decide so will you see.
–ACIM (Text, 12, VII, 7, 11)

The *internal* feelings, thoughts, and beliefs that we are ignoring the most are the ones most likely to be observed and/or experienced in the *external* world. This would, of course, include the reflections of our inner conditions that we project onto those people closest to us, such as our partners. What most people fail to understand is that these reflections can be either *positive* or *negative*. In either case, though, **our job is to Recognize our projections and bring them back into ourselves, so we can "own" them and learn what they are trying to teach us.**

When these projections are mirroring, or reflecting, *positive* messages or traits of ourselves onto others (as with persons whom we admire or find attractive), they reveal traits either that we *have,* but are denying OR traits we need to *nurture*, but are thus far failing to do so. Therefore, by projecting these traits onto someone in the outer world, our souls (higher selves) are hoping that our human (lower) selves will take the hint and become so attracted to these traits that we will nurture them and/or claim them for ourselves.

Conversely, when these projections are mirroring, or reflecting, *negative* messages, issues, or traits of ourselves onto others (as with persons who irritate or repulse us), they show us issues that we may dislike in ourselves and/or are trying to avoid. And, as in the example given for *positive* mirroring, by projecting these issues onto people in the outer world, our souls are hoping that our human selves will eventually get so annoyed by these negative traits that we no longer can avoid our unhealed wounds (triggered by these traits) that are in need of forgiveness and release.

In the case of *negative* mirroring, it is often our most *intimate* relationships that assist us the most in healing by uncovering our deepest fears, judgments, doubts, and insecurities. **We may be able to ignore or hide from these issues while living alone, but when we choose to interact closely with others, as in an intimate relationship, it is nearly impossible to ignore our hidden issues.** However, we rarely will jump at the chance to Recognize the opportunity before us. Most people do not have the courage to Recognize that if someone is upsetting them, it is not so much what the other person is saying or doing (or failing to say or do) that is causing an issue, as it is that the other person is merely triggering an unhealed wound which already exists within us. Ironically, **we probably would remain unaware of the issues lurking in the deep recesses of our souls or subconscious selves were it not for the people who mirror negative traits to us.**

If, however, this concept of mirroring is not acceptable to you, there is another perspective worth considering. You could ask yourself if it is easier to change the other people in your life who are triggering negative feelings in you OR easier to heal or change yourself. This compelling question might make it possible to Accept the idea of your being, at least partly, responsible for whom (and what) you attract into your life and then choosing to do something about it, thus changing whatever it is in you that originally drew such people into your life. When you change the source (cause), you will most certainly change the outcome (effect).

> *Turn on, turn in, turn your eyes around.*
> *Look at yourself, Look at yourself.*
>
> **–Strawberry Alarm Clock**
> (Song: "Incense and Peppermints")

Again, the concept of mirroring is a universal law that says, **"Whatever you see outside of yourself is a reflection (mirror) of what is happening on the inside."** This law is either true or not true. It isn't true *sometimes* or only when we want it to be. Whatever we see in the realm of form is the manifestation of our *thoughts* and *beliefs*. Nothing in the world can manifest by accident or on its own. Instead, it is the result of *thoughts* and *beliefs* held individually and/or collectively. More specifically, *thought* is the *active* principle behind creation, but *belief* is the *passive* principle behind creation. Although it is a popular notion that our thoughts primarily create our reality or experience; in truth, our *thoughts* are much like military generals who merely put into motion the directions given by their leader. It is the *beliefs* held within our souls that "call the shots" and create the lives we live.

Besides having two versions—positive and negative—mirroring also takes one of two forms: literal or symbolic. It is easier for most people to see the *literal* form of mirroring: where something outside of you manifests as a literal reflection of your thought or belief. For example, manifesting a controlling person in your life may mirror that you, yourself, are *literally* a controlling person and that you need to heal or observe this tendency. *Symbolic* mirroring, on the other hand, rarely reflects anything of *literal* significance. In such a case, you may have a controlling person in your life, but it is clear that you are in no way a controlling person yourself. So, why then, are you manifesting a controlling person in your life and what could he or she be reflecting to you? You have to look within yourself to discern the "*symbolic*" meaning. When you ask yourself what "controlling" people symbolize (or mean) to you, you may find that they evoke "insecurity" in you or perhaps a "fear of authority" (control).

It could be then, that it is either this insecurity or the fear of authority that needs healing, rather than a literal tendency to be controlling.

Truly understanding the law and concept of mirroring requires accepting the fact that all things are somehow connected and that **whatever manifests *externally*, always originates *internally*.** Understanding this law also requires taking yourself to a whole new level of responsibility by accepting that all things seen, felt, or experienced are merely a means of meeting yourself.

As an evolved and responsible being, you will not want to miss a chance to heal and move to a higher level of consciousness. You will understand how crucial it is to see all things as mirrors, or reflections, of something inside calling for learning or healing. You will choose to answer that call by seeing through the healing lens of forgiveness.

When you meet anyone, remember it is a holy encounter. As you see him [or her] you will see yourself. As you treat him you will treat yourself. As you think of him you will think of yourself. Never forget this, for in him you will find yourself or lose yourself. . . . Give him his place in the Kingdom and you will have yours.

–ACIM (Text 8, III)

Chapter 6

WHY SOME PEOPLE DON'T HEAL

If the subject of this book were the human body and human illnesses, it might be said that there are *many* reasons why people don't heal. They could, for example, be misdiagnosed or forget to take their medication, or they could be taking the *wrong* medication. Then, again, perhaps the unhealed patients are simply too far advanced in their illnesses and *beyond* help or the possibility of recovering. But these are all matters concerning *physical* healing that have little or nothing to do with the focus of this book.

Instead, this book is concerned with healing the heart and soul. Therefore, we are dealing with the internal, psychological, and spiritual blocks that keep people from healing. Ultimately, these various internal blocks are mere masks of the ego attempting to hide our true selves and true potentials.

The human ego could be defined as the name given to our belief in limitation, our low self-esteem, or our

collective belief that we are separate from God (which we are not, despite the way we sometimes feel). The ego (our belief in separation) then, is the fundamental cause for those moments in our lives when we experience a lack of healing (or a lack of anything else for that matter—money, happiness, health, relationship, etc.).

> *Each day* . . . [when you experience hurt, hate, illness, or lack] *you but relive the single instant when the time of terror* [the mistaken belief that we are separated from God] *took the place of love.*
> –ACIM (Text 26, VI)

Experiencing blocks to our greater good not only wears on us but sometimes becomes unbearable when we begin to witness the effects in our lives. To complicate matters, our personal pain is often increased proportionately to the increasing growth in our awareness of these blocks. **Once we begin to wake up, there is no going back.** When we begin to learn to recognize our issues, it is nearly impossible to escape them or avoid working on them—especially when we have seen the benefits of "doing the work."

> *The greater the light, the darker the shadow.*
> –**Anonymous**

To further complicate this battle, as we experience personal awakening to any degree, we no longer "get away with" some of the ego-centered behaviors as we once did. Now, because of our increased light of understanding, our spiritual conscience will no longer allow us to skirt around and ignore our mistakes or issues. Therefore, we feel their consequences almost immediately. Now, **"instant karma" begins to replace the old, long-term payment plan often referred to as "reincarnation."** This surfacing of instant karma may cause us to long for the days when we were less consciously aware—the days when we were numb to the issues that are now closing in on us. But, **our hearts can be lifted by knowing that there is a reason for difficult times—even the ones that are recurring patterns in our lives.**

During these, and all times of difficulty, it would be helpful to remind yourself of one or more of these following uplifting principles. First, despite the seeming weight of your difficulty, "this too shall pass," meaning that most of the time, such tests last only for a little while. Next, know that **despite outward appearances, a perfect image of love, compassion, and peace exists deep down in the core of your being.** Remind yourself that occasionally these issues return for you to look at them from a higher, more healed perspective. Also remember that everyone accepts at least one cross, or issue, to bear in order to remain dense enough to stay embodied. Therefore, when you've done all you can to heal a particular issue but to no avail, it sometimes helps to practice "Accepting" the cross (issue), rather than resisting or obsessing over it.

Of course, this cross is often a relationship with another person in our lives. As we process through our chosen/given issues, we begin merging with our true, divine nature. At this point in our Soul-Level Healing, we often reach a state of mind referred to in *A Course in Miracles*, as the day **we start feeling grateful to those who seem to have hurt us badly enough to force us to go within and embark on the path of Soul-Level Healing**. Moreover, it is only by gathering the faith and strength to commit to healing our "stuff" that we are able to enter the "peace that surpasses understanding"—God Consciousness.

Whenever the cross you bear causes you to remain unhealed (meaning that you knowingly or unknowingly still allow your past to control, or influence, you in a way that feels hurtful), then you will find yourself incapable of feeling, experiencing, or extending the unconditional love that brings you peace, true forgiveness, and fulfillment. Nevertheless, even though you may feel that you have "had enough of this" and are tired of the grief that some past trauma has caused you—possibly to the point of wanting to "give up"—if you do nothing to heal this issue, it will continue to haunt you. Therefore, you must stay the course and remain vigilant on your path of inner healing.

You can learn to see "the cross you bear" as a focal point for healing through forgiveness—not only to release yourself but also to release everyone else on the planet with a similar issue. As it is done in one of us, it is done, to some degree, in all.

> *When I am healed I am not healed alone.*
> **–ACIM** (Les. 137)

To accomplish the goal of healing, we need to Accept that there is a purpose (usually beyond human awareness) for any particular crosses (or issues) being in our lives. We need to "own up" to the fact that on some level, we signed-on for this assignment. Once we Accept these basic principles, we can feel empowered once again, knowing we now can choose a *different* direction, rather than remaining frozen in a stalemate and/or continuing on as victims.

As we release "victimhood," we can bid farewell to our victimizers. Oddly enough, this concept is frightening for many of us. After all, we may have had these people ("victimizers") in our lives for a long time. We may be afraid of what life would be like without them or the pain that they share with us. As we seek to do the inner healing necessary for spiritual advancement, we all would do well to take an honest look within to see if this possibility applies to us. Otherwise, we are bound to repeat the same patterns of the past—since we often underestimate how programmed we may be in this and other areas.

For example, a study was once done with newborn kittens. When the kittens began to open their eyes, they were separated into a controlled environment consisting of two groups. The first group was put in a box with horizontal stripes; the second group, in a box with vertical stripes. After several days of allowing their sight (visual programming) to develop, they were let loose into a normal environment. It was discovered immediately that the kittens could see only what they had previously been programmed to see. Therefore, the first group couldn't see such vertical objects as the legs of a chair, and the second group couldn't see horizontal objects. This same principle holds true for all of us. We are far too prone to seeing only what our past limited and/or unhealthy programs allow us to see. The only remedy is to change these programs by healing them.

An important aspect to healing limiting, unhealthy programs is the understanding that **true healing is a two-sided coin that involves dealing with our old wounds AND learning to focus on the joy of the New Life we are creating.** We have to know when it is time to focus on Emptying of the past (Recognize, Accept, and Surrender) and when it is time to shift gears and begin welcoming a New Life (Refill and Give Thanks). In other words, instead of attempting to heal by constantly dealing with our old wounds, we also have to spend sufficient time focusing on the light at the end of the healing tunnel.

Reaching this point of enjoying your New Life may sound attractive and easy, but to attain this stage takes much commitment and personal discipline—as there are people, hurts, programs, and patterns calling you back to the past. However, **with sufficient commitment to your goal, you will discover that you can heal and release the past (and all its inhabitants), as well as the control it once had over you.** These moments of change and choice are made easier when you create and use healthy support systems (friends, counselors, etc.) and the many practical tools/techniques (healers, healing arts, etc.) available to assist through the healing process.

Eventually, as you approach the "light at the end of the tunnel," you will encounter signs that you are healing. One of the most affirming signs of healing is found in the altering of negative *feelings* (such as anger and pain) and negative *actions* (such as impatience and hurtful words or behaviors).

When you truly have gone through the Soul-Level Healing Process, the memories or people involved no longer find buttons inside of you to push. Having fewer reactions, though, is not enough, since we all can become masters at suppressing and denying our responses. Instead, the ultimate sign of healing is found in a heightened sense of peace in the face of the previously upsetting memories or pain—or their manifestation in present circumstances. You might be surprised to find that you not only have little or no reaction to the old "stuff," but you actually feel PEACEFUL despite it all; peace has replaced your pain. **You will know you are healed when old issues have as little effect on you as a light breeze has on a well-rooted tree.**

We will feel the pain or effects of our hurts until we choose to release them. And choose we must! We can't have both—hurting *and* healing. One or the other of these alternatives will dominate our consciousness and therefore our lives. The one that is stronger will continuously download its effects into our lives, much like a computer program that is set to run automatically. Unfortunately, unhealthy programs are easier to set up to run automatically, while healthy programs often have to be consistently *chosen*. Unfair as this might seem, it is the way we have established this system in our minds and souls.

As long as we continue to wrestle with our past wounds, our egos will create clever obstacles to healing. These obstacles are really just psychological patterns or belief systems that keep us from experiencing a sudden, dramatic shift, or healing, away from whatever seems to be bothering us or causing us pain. These ego-created obstacles are as follows:

1. **FEAR**—If you are afraid of healing, healing will not occur. Of course most people would say it is absurd to think that anyone would be afraid of healing. Nevertheless, it is true. Healing sometimes means letting go of your all too familiar past and your most ingrained patterns. Also, when healing takes the form of miraculous changes or manifestations, such as altering physical laws, it can sometimes intimidate any witnesses, including you. If you were told that your problem or disease was caused by a horrible incident from the past that you would rather not remember (and that your healing was contingent upon remembering), you may find yourself too fearful and, therefore, may not experience a healing. Some people even fail to heal because they fear any form of healing that conflicts with their religious and/or family beliefs.

2. **ANGER**—Anger is perhaps the most commonly overlooked reason that people don't heal. Anger can inhibit healing because obsessing on the anger (or on whoever or whatever hurt you and made you angry) leaves little room for a shift into love, forgiveness, and the miracle of healing. Choosing to

remain angry (and it is indeed a choice) is essentially the same as saying, "I refuse to let this issue go or let that person off the hook." Such a decision is sure to keep the problem or illness alive. In fact, the problem or illness "feeds" off of the anger trapped within your consciousness, as well as within your body.

3. **DENIAL**—Denial is one of the primary defenses that prevent healing for any person. If you attempt to deny, minimize or rationalize your woundedness from this or any other lifetime, you are automatically setting a limit as to how far and how deeply you are willing to heal. Of course, all aspects of denial are rooted in a combination of fear, guilt, and/or shame.

4. **BELIEVING YOU ARE ALREADY HEALED**—This block to healing is the "been there, done that" attitude, whereby people think that since they've already done some work on a particular issue, they are "done" and need not do any more healing. Such thinking is "control based" and is what lies behind so many addicts reverting to their old habitual behavior. Such individuals think they've done enough healing and are ready to move on. However, they learn the hard way that, although they may feel they are done with their issues, their issues aren't done with them. It's better to remind yourself that most healing is not an *event* that occurs at the snap of a finger but, instead, is a *process* that takes time.

5. **CONTROL**—The need to control people, your life, your environment, and your destiny is indeed reason enough to stay stuck in whatever health or personal challenge you may be experiencing. The need to control usually arises from a mixture of *fear* and *anger*. If you are afraid, you will feel compelled to protect yourself and attempt to control your environment. If you are angry, you will feel compelled to fight against (or control) whatever threat you perceive—even if the threat is merely the slightest opportunity to let go of the past and allow healing. The person who insists on controlling the rate of their healing, however, perceives the concept of "letting go" as a sign of weakness and, therefore, needs to maintain control, or hold on to, their hurt and anger—even if it kills them.

6. **DOUBT**—This is probably one of the most insidious blocks to healing. Doubt can occur consciously or unconsciously and can take the form of our own thoughts and verbalizations, or it can come from other people's influences. Although we may have our own set of doubts that are haunting us and attempting to slow down our progress, doubt often comes riding into our lives on the backs of those whom we refer to as friends, healers, partners, or family members. Doubt will nearly always try to sabotage

a "good thing." For example, we may experience a shift for the better only to allow the doubts imposed by others to creep in and spoil the flow of the miracle. Sometimes doubts enter our minds because we feel unworthy to receive healing. Other times, we may doubt the healing technique, thinking it is impossible for a healer using an unconventional method of healing to accomplish what previous healers or physicians could not. Or, a doubt may creep in concerning the healer—often taking the form of experiencing a healing but having "others" plant a doubt in our minds regarding the healer's abilities or even the healer's character. What happens is that we experience something new and wonderful in our lives, and the ego does everything in its power to make us doubt this change. Our healing is blocked by doubt, and of course, we are back to where we started or even worse off than before, since now we have added the conscious anger toward whoever failed to heal us or the unconscious guilt we feel for ruining our opportunity for a true healing. If such an unfortunate situation befalls us, we need to see it for what it is. Although others may be involved in "raining on our parade," **ultimately we are responsible for both the doubts that we are attracting AND our responses to these doubts.** Furthermore, it is up to us to make a determined decision to say "NO" to such doubts, as well as forgive ourselves for having created these doubts and paying attention to them. We then need to move forward by making plans to get back on track, get back to our healing work, and choose again.

7. **LACK OF FORGIVENESS**—Although this final block to healing is an overlap of many of the previously mentioned reasons people don't heal, it is, nonetheless, worth mentioning. **If you fail to completely forgive someone or something, you cannot heal completely**. It doesn't matter if you claim to have not known that forgiveness was necessary or that you simply forgot to do it. Both of these excuses are subtle forms of control and provide a means for remaining unhealed.

In summary, if you feel you cannot bear looking at something that needs healing, you are in *fear*. If you refuse to forgive, you are in *anger*. If you think you are "just fine" and have nobody to forgive, you are in *denial*. If you think you've already forgiven, despite the fact that something is clearly upsetting your life, you are in the attitude that *you've already healed*. If you choose to wait until other people in your life acknowledge their "misdeeds" and apologize before you will grant them forgiveness, you are exhibiting obvious signs of *control*. Lastly, if you allow *doubt* to creep in, you are obviously listening to a voice that wants you to fail in your healing. These various reasons you do not heal might look different, but in the final analysis, they are all the same. They are all forms of refusing to choose a life of love, healing, and forgiveness.

If you understand and Accept these aforementioned reasons for not healing, it should be easier to catch yourself when you are consciously or unconsciously avoiding healing. If you truly want to heal at the level of the heart and soul, which is synonymous with forgiving, you will come to Accept that you cannot continue to (1) be fearful, (2) be angry, (3) be in denial, (4) believe you're already healed, (5) be in control, (6) have doubts, and/or (7) choose to withhold forgiveness. Instead, you will choose to humbly *Recognize* there is a problem. You will then *Accept* that you are still angry and hurt inside. Next, you will prayerfully *Surrender* the old wounds to Spirit (God); you will *Refill* the newly emptied spaces with positive, revitalizing beliefs; and lastly you will *Give Thanks*. This formula—the solution to resolving your blocks to healing—is an expression of the five steps of the Soul-Level Healing Process.

Chapter 7

THE ROLE
OF A HEALER

Before covering the primary concepts behind be-ing an effective healer, a few important guidelines need to be established: If you are truly being a channel of healing or life transformation for another person, it means that you are (1) recognizing that God (Spirit) is the only true Source of the healing; (2) holding the intention to be a channel of forgiveness and miraculous blessings, as well as maintaining the proper attitude and mind-set of a healer; and (3) following, as closely as possible, a procedure that takes your client, friend, or yourself through as many stages as possible of a complete healing process—such as the Soul-Level Healing Process. If you follow these three major guidelines, the fact that you are a healer cannot be questioned.

Another important fact to remember (but not an essential aspect to the work) is that if you practice the above outlined steps for being a true healer, it also means you fit into a category referred to as a "miracle worker." Of course, to think of yourself as a miracle worker might bring up such issues as thinking you are being arrogant or overrating your skills. But these ego-related issues will not be a problem if you keep in mind that it is not *you* who does the healing work, nor is it *your* skills that facilitate the healing and the outcome. It is *God*!

> *Those who follow the path of service, who have completely purified themselves and conquered their . . . self-will, see the Self in all creatures and . . . think always, 'I am not the doer.'.*
>
> **–The Bhagavad Gita** (Chapt. 5)

Therefore, as long as you recognize that you are merely a "channel" of the healing, then who are you to question the Source, the means, and the effectiveness of the healing? Conversely, if you say that you are *not* a miracle worker, then you are affirming that *no* miracle is being created. Consequently, why should you or your client or friend expect to *see* a miracle? Furthermore, why should people (clients) come to see you and pay you as a professional if you are offering anything less than a miraculous shift—on one level or another?

*Whenever a . . . [healer, or miracle worker] has
tried to be a channel for healing he has succeed-
ed. Should he [or she] be tempted to doubt this
. . . he must use his reason to tell himself that he
has given the problem to One Who cannot fail,
and must recognize that his own uncertainty is
not love but fear [and doubt].*
–ACIM (Manual 7, 2)

The following are the steps and guidelines for developing the ability to be an effective healer, as well as for
becoming a more loving and forgiving person, which
again, is synonymous with becoming a more effective
healer. It should be noted, however, that since healing is
ultimately an act of forgiveness (or the desire to change
our opinions or perceptions), nearly all guidelines and
comments made here are relevant (and can also be applied) to all forms of relationships including those with
clients, friends, partners, family members, and even
people we pass on the street or have never met.

The majority of the quotes in this chapter are taken
from *A Course in Miracles* and the related booklet *Psychotherapy: Purpose, Process, and Practice*. What follows are suggestions for healers, or anyone committed
to practicing the art of healing and/or forgiveness. And
since we are all potentially healers (provided we are

committed to seeing others as healthy and whole), the people with whom we practice these principles will be referred to as "clients."

I. **Recognize that God (Spirit) is the only true Source of the healing.**

1. **Our Source for healing, Spirit, acts as our Guide in everything: from whoever has been guided to meet us to whatever we do when they arrive:** There are no chance meetings or accidental encounters. "Everyone who is sent to you is a client of yours. This does not mean that you select him [or her], nor that *you* choose the kind of treatment that is suitable. Who, then, decides what each client needs? Surely not you." But God, within *your mind,* and the mind of your client will guide you as to what to do if you listen. But you must practice listening.

2. **As a healer, or miracle worker, you are learning to surrender to your employer (Spirit/God):** This surrendering will probably require changes in your mind and soul (your belief systems), which "may or may not involve changes in the external situation." As the healer, or miracle worker, advances in his (or her) training, he learns one lesson with increasing thoroughness: He does not make his own decisions; he asks his Teacher

(God/Spirit) for His answer, and it is this he follows as his guide for action. This asking for guidance becomes easier and easier. There is no standard routine, for the lessons change each day. He will be told all that his role should be, this day and every day. Broadly speaking, then, it can be said that it is well to start the day right by asking for guidance. And remember, it is always possible to begin again, should the day begin with error.

3. **God (our Guide in the healing process of all minds) is who we are:** When all minds are healed and forgiven and returned to their original state of Divinity, we will discover that the God we relied upon as a Guide was really just a part of ourselves—the part of us that never forgot who we really are. "The glory of [God] is my own . . . Let not the truth about ourselves today be hidden by a false humility . . . We thank You [God] for the light that shines forever in us. And we honor it, because You share it with us. We are one, united in this light and one with You, at peace with all creation and ourselves."

II. **Hold the intention to be a channel of forgiveness and miraculous blessings, as well as to maintain the proper attitude and mindset of a healer.**

1. **The healer and client are one and the same:** Although we are all ultimately equal, it is appropriate that some of us assume the role of healer while others assume the role of client. These roles will change from time to time. But both healer and client must inevitably trust in something greater than themselves. "The healer is a leader in the sense that he [or she] walks slightly ahead of the client, and helps him to avoid a few of the pitfalls along the road. Ideally, he is also a follower, for [Spirit] should walk ahead of him to give him light to see. Without this [Divine Guide], both will merely stumble blindly on." The healer must recognize the equality of himself and the client. "No one is healed alone. This is the joyous song salvation sings to all who hear its Voice. This statement cannot be too often remembered by healers." Their clients can but be seen as "the bringers of forgiveness, for it is they who come to demonstrate their true perfection to eyes that still believe that false belief systems are there to look upon. Yet will the proof of true perfection, seen in the client and accepted in the healer, offer the mind of both a covenant in which they meet and join and are as one."

2. **A healer, or miracle worker, is anyone who chooses to be one:** As with all things in life, to

be a healer is a choice—one that reflects a person's decision to shift from living life as a victim to becoming a student of truth. Furthermore, becoming a healer, or miracle worker, is a choice to become a master—a representative of Spirit on earth. "Once he [or she] has done that [made this choice], his road is established and his direction is sure. He has entered an agreement with God. He has become a healer or miracle worker." The word "healer" here does not refer to only those who are licensed professionals (counselors, doctors, massage therapists, etc.). Although a healer might be a specialist in some form, all people who have chosen to assist themselves and others in experiencing a shift, or healing, of their minds and souls (from crisis or pain to peace and healing) are healers.

3. **You do not need to be "perfect" to be a healer and miracle worker:** The ego need not be completely healed or eliminated in order to be an effective healer or even to reach enlightenment. In fact, while you are in a body, you actually *need* at least a fragment of an ego left to maintain the visibility of a physical form. Otherwise, you would actually turn (re-turn) into Light. More important than being perfect (especially

based on human standards), or without ego, is that you set aside your ego—if even for a moment—to allow the Perfection of Spirit to flow through you. Miracles are expressions of miracle-mindedness, and "miracle-mindedness" means "right-mindedness," or maintaining a loving, forgiving mind demonstrated by kindness to others. "However, as a correction, the miracle need not await the right-mindedness of the intended receiver [your client, friend, or family member]. In fact, its purpose is to restore him *to* his right mind. It is essential, however, that you, the healer or miracle worker, be in your right mind, however briefly, or you will be unable to re-establish right-mindedness in someone else. The healer who relies on his own readiness is endangering his understanding. You are perfectly safe as long as you are completely unconcerned about your readiness." Instead, maintain a consistent trust in God's. "When your miracle working inclinations are not functioning properly, it is always because fear has intruded on your right-mindedness and has turned it upside down," which is always a sign that you have somehow refused to accept the healing of your own mind.

4. **A true healer has a unique way of perceiving his/ her client:** True healers, or miracle workers, nev-

er focus on the many forms of sickness in which their brothers believe. Their clients do not realize that it is *they* who have chosen sickness. "On the contrary, they believe that sickness has chosen them." As far as they know, "the body tells them what to do and they obey." "A sick person perceives himself as separate from God. Would you see him as separate from you? It is your task to heal the sense of separation that has made him sick. It is your function to recognize for him that what he believes about himself is not the truth. It is your forgiveness that must show him this." "To them [the sick] the separation is quite real," which means that people who are sick perceive themselves as separate from God, the Source of all hope and healing, and therefore believe themselves to be powerless against all illness and trauma. The true healer "seeks for God's Voice in this brother." And the true healer reminds his client "that he did not make himself, and [therefore] must remain as God created him," perfect and whole. The truth in the mind of the healer reaches out to the truth in the minds of their friends or clients. These clients are thus "brought to truth; truth is not brought to them. And this is the function of God's [healers]; to see no will as separate from their own, nor theirs as separate from God's. Nor is it at this level that the healer calls forth the miracle of healing. He overlooks the mind and body, seeing only the face of Christ shining in front of him, correcting all mistakes and healing all perception." This is being in our right, Divine, Mind. "This realization is the final goal of [true healing]. How is it reached? The [healer] sees in the [client] all that he has not forgiven in himself, and is thus given another chance to look at it, open it to re-evaluation and forgive it." When this forgiveness occurs, the healer sees his previous false belief as disappearing into a past that no longer exists. The client is merely the healer's screen for the projection of those past beliefs, demonstrating the essential equality of the minds of the healer and client.

5. **What to do when the appearance of healing is not present:** At one time or another, all healers are confronted with the issue of not being able to perceive the healing they intend to channel. This experience can bring up seemingly serious or distressing doubt concerning one's work. Nevertheless, "no true healer should feel disappointed if he [or she] has offered healing and it does not appear to have been received. It is not up to him to judge when his gift should be accepted. Let him be

certain it has been received, and trust that it will be accepted when it is recognized as a blessing and not a curse." At this point, the healer needs to tactfully instruct the client that it is right, safe, and possible to heal and bid farewell to that which has made him previously feel bound. These moments also present an opportunity for the healer to recognize issues held within his own unhealed mind. "When a teacher [or healer] of God fails to heal [their client], it is because he has forgotten Who he is. Another's sickness thus [reflects] his own . . . In so doing, he has refused to accept the Atonement for himself, and can hardly offer it to his brother in Christ's Name." Nevertheless, when evidence of healing is not forthcoming, should the healing be repeated more than once for the exact same issue? "This question really answers itself . . . If [all true] healing is certain, as we have already said it is, [then] what is there to repeat?" In other words, although the healer might not see the results, yet, all true healing is certain. Therefore the healer can always rest assured that his job is done. Any thought to the contrary stems from his own ego, thus revealing where he himself can use some healing. "And it is this he must facilitate. He [the healer] is now the client, and he must so regard himself. He has made a mistake, and must be willing to change his mind about it. He lacked trust . . . and so he has not received the benefit of his gift."

6. **Sometimes a healer channels miracles through words and often takes the role of a "teacher:"** A healer or teacher of God must learn to use words in a new way. Gradually, he [or she] learns not to speak but instead, allows words to be spoken through him. He becomes merely a channel and lets his words be chosen for him. "The teacher of God accepts the words which are offered him, and gives as he receives. He does not control the direction of his speaking. He listens and hears and speaks. A major hindrance is the teacher of God's fear about the validity of what he hears. And what he hears may indeed be quite startling. It may also seem to be quite irrelevant to the presented problem and may, in fact, be very embarrassing to him. All these are judgments that have no value. They are his own, coming from a shabby self-perception which he would leave behind. Judge not the words that come to you, but offer them in confidence."

III. **Follow, as closely as possible, a procedure that takes your client, friend, or yourself through as**

many stages as possible of a complete healing process—such as the Soul-Level Healing Process. Also,
there are some specific things you must remember
about those who are brought to you for healing.

1. **The only true healing is healing of the mind, but
   what if you or your friend or client is not yet suf-
   ficiently advanced to use exclusively the mind to
   heal?:** Know the truth (that you are healthy and
   whole), but respect the illusion (that until you
   completely understand and accept the truth of
   who you are, you might need some assistance in
   your healing). "Physical medications are forms of
   'spells'," but if you are not yet ready or able to
   exclusively "use the mind to heal, you should *not*
   attempt to do so. The very fact that you are afraid
   [or unprepared in any way] makes your mind
   vulnerable" to creating greater problems. You are
   therefore unlikely to accept the real Source of the
   healing, nor the real source of the problem. When
   these conditions are present, "it is safer for you
   to rely temporarily" on some form of healing tool
   (herb, aspirin, massage, surgery, etc.). For now,
   these external tools are familiar and are something in which you can believe.

2. **Since a true healing or miracle can occur only in
   the "present" moment, it often entails erasing the**

past (traumas and beliefs): When the past is unhealed, it typically causes what could be referred
to as "age regressions," wherein the clients' past
wounds drag them back in time (usually in unconscious ways) to somehow feel or relive their
original traumas. Conversely, when the past is
healed (or "in the process" of healing), it typically
causes what could be referred to as "time conver-
gences." In other words, all time is drawn together
into one single moment (a holy instant), the past
being brought forward for the purpose of healing
and release. "A miracle enables you to see your
brother without his past, and so perceive him as
born again. His errors are all past, and by perceiving him without them you are releasing him. And
since his past is yours, you share in this release."

3. **Healing can be channeled over long-distances:**
Although there are numerous healing arts that
apply the use of long-distance healing as part of
their curriculum, few healers understand how
such healing is accomplished. If, for example,
you as the healer imagine your client is in a different time or location from you and then send
the client healing, you might have some success.
However, the fact that you believe there is a time
or distance for your healing to travel will limit

the effectiveness of the healing. Instead, for long-distance healing to be truly understood and most effective, it is necessary to accept that there is no such thing as time and space (as we know it). All is here and now! Therefore, your client is *with* you and in fact *is* you. Knowing this truth will ensure greater success in long-distance healing. "Your [clients] need not be physically present for you to serve them. This may be hard to remember, but Spirit will not have Its gifts of Love and Healing limited to the few you actually see. Some do not need your physical presence. It does not matter how they come. They will be sent in whatever form is most helpful; a name, a thought, a picture, an idea, or perhaps just a feeling." Even if a mere thought or image of a person crosses your mind (or even your television or computer screen), it might very well be a call for healing.

4. **God is the Source of the healing, but your mind is the channel of the healing:** Since it is the mind and its stored false belief systems that are sick and in need of healing, it must also be "the mind" that becomes the channel for every form of healing—seen and unseen. When you (or your client) create *effective* healers and healings, it is because your mind is ready to create such. The same

holds true when you create *ineffective* healers
and healings. These are all merely manifestations
of what you believe you are ready to accept or
experience. And, ironically, none of these healers
or tools is actually needed. "The [client] could
merely rise up without the assistance of anyone
or anything else [if he would but believe] and say,
'I have no use for this.' There . . . [would then be]
. . . no form of sickness that would not be cured
at once."

5. **The body and its symptoms can be viewed as messengers that tell us what kinds of issues are going on in the mind:** The body might indeed be what
many refer to as an illusion, but it still holds one
very important value—being a signpost of where
we are going wrong in our thinking and belief
systems. The body, therefore, can reveal specifics of areas where we have ignored or withheld
forgiveness and missed an opportunity for healing. "Sickness takes many forms, and so does unforgiveness. The forms of one but reproduce the
forms of the other, for they are the same illusion.
So closely is one translated into the other, that
a careful study of the form a sickness takes will
point quite clearly to the form of un-forgiveness
that it represents." If, for example, a person ex-

periences an inner issue (somewhere in his or her soul) involving the concept of hearing (such as not being willing to hear advice from others), it could very well literally manifest as a physical issue related to the ears or hearing. "Yet seeing this [on an intellectual level] will not effect a cure." This is achieved only through forgiveness and Soul-Level Healing.

6. **To charge or not to charge (for healing), that is the question:** It is impossible to put a financial value on work that heals the soul, for the soul has little or no value to the material world, and the material world has little or no value to the soul. Furthermore, since the healer, or miracle worker, is demonstrating in consciousness that Spirit is the Source behind the healing (and Spirit freely gives the healing), a value cannot be placed on this work. Nevertheless, since Spirit does indeed desire to see people healed and released from the pain of their false belief systems, even God encourages the healer to charge for his work ("the laborer is worthy of his reward" –The Bible, I Timothy 5:18). Financial reimbursement helps the healer continue on—although sometimes money is not the reward needed or given as assistance. However, "one rule should always be

observed: No one should be turned away because he cannot pay."

So do we lay aside our amulets, our charms and medicines, our chants and bits of magic [various physical and emotional healing arts] *in whatever form they take. We will be still and listen for the Voice of healing, Which will cure all ills as one . . . No Voice* [Thing] *but This can* [truly] *cure.*

—ACIM (Les. 140)

PART TWO

Soul-Level Healing:
The Process

Chapter 8

THE FIVE STEPS TO
SOUL-LEVEL HEALING

The steps used for Soul-Level Healing may be referred to by different names; however, Soul-Level Healing always involves some form of (1) *Recognizing* there is a problem, (2) *Accepting* that there are deeper issues than those known to have created the problem, (3) *Surrendering* the problem with all its aspects, symptoms, and relevant people to God, (4) *Refilling* or replacing the previous problem and hidden causes with something new—God's Presence, and (5) *Giving Thanks* for all that has been healed or transformed— even before observed externally.

Although there are five steps within the Soul-Level Healing Process (experiencing a true healing or shift in consciousness), each step can be seen as a process unto itself and can be powerful and cathartic. For some people, the first step (Recognizing they have a problem) may be the most powerful of all. For other people, it may be the deeper insights into themselves gained in the second step (Acceptance of the deeper issues behind the problem) that could prove the most powerful of all the steps. Yet, for others, the third step (Surrendering their issues or problems) may be the most powerful. And still for others it could be the fourth or the fifth step that proves most powerful.

Again, any single step can be very transforming for your life, but all five combined will bring the most profound and permanent results. Therefore, any process of true healing—soul healing—should involve all five steps. Most of the finest healers on the planet use at least a few of these steps, although not necessarily calling them by the same name. For example, the healing technique known as EFT (Emotional Freedom Technique) may *appear* to involve only a special technique of reprogramming (or Refilling) the body-mind and not include the other four steps necessary for Soul-Level Healing. Nevertheless, this well-known process (EFT) does much more. It asks the recipients to identify (Recognize) their problems and sometimes suggests that they look deeper to see if there are underlying issues that also need clearing (Accept). The EFT process then encourages a step of releasing (Surrender) through tapping on specific acupuncture points of the body, which creates (Refill) a sense of calm or peace for the recipient. The EFT process usually ends here, missing only the final step (Giving Thanks).

Although EFT clearly incorporates most of the five steps of Soul-Level Healing, the steps within that healing art can be deepened in their effectiveness and power by making them more "spiritual." To accomplish this, while tapping the acu-points of the body, or perhaps when the EFT process is nearly completed, the recipient could choose to invoke, or "call in" the Power and Presence of God/Spirit and then close the session by Giving Thanks. Just this minor adjustment to an already effective healing technique will transform it into a more complete Soul-Level Healing Process.

The five steps of Soul-Level Healing are a symbolic movement of the soul through each of the five levels of human consciousness (physical, emotional, intellectual, intuitive, and spiritual). This, in turn, symbolizes a movement through each of the five elements (earth, water, fire, air, and ether). As you progress through the five steps of healing, you also travel through all major states of consciousness, since each step aligns with one of the five levels of human consciousness and initiations (life's tests) that correspond to the five elements. This means that the step of *Recognizing* your primary problem mostly relates to your physical, material life. The step of *Accepting* relates mostly to your emotions.

The step of *Surrendering* relates mostly to your mind and intellect. The step of *Refilling* relates mostly to your heart and soul. Finally, the Step of *Giving Thanks* relates mostly to your Spirit.

In an effort to help liberate us from a world of wounds and old, negative patterns, *A Course in Miracles* reminds us what must be done to become free from the issues that bind us. Rather than keeping our "heads in the clouds" and merely using "positive thinking" in an attempt to transform any pressing issue, the *Course* tells us that the problem first must be "identified" and then must be "let go" *before* it can be "replaced." The first two of these steps mentioned in the Course are referred to in the Soul-Level Healing Process as three steps: "Recognizing," "Accepting," and "Surrendering." The *Course* further insists that these "first two steps of this process (of *identifying* and *letting go* of the problem) require our cooperation." We are then advised to add the third and final step, which is to "replace" whatever it was that we released. To prepare for this final step, the Voice in *A Course in Miracles* is adamant that we *first* have to do an adequate amount of healing and taking responsibility to heal the wounds in our soul *before* Spirit can bring us the gifts of A New Life.

This final step of the manifestation of A New Life, according to the *Course*, will not "need our cooperation" (in other words, "Let go and let God"), for **miracle working is not attempting, or trying, to *make* something happen; it is *allowing* Spirit to pour into our souls and bring us what has been there all along— Love, Peace, Joy, and Abundance.**

> *I will step back and let* [God] *lead the way.*
> –ACIM (Les. 155)

The full *three* steps for healing an issue, referred to in *A Course in Miracles* (and further divided into *five* steps in the Soul-Level Healing Process), are comparable to the various steps of personal transformation found in Taoism or Buddhism and even in the "12-Step Program." All of these thought-systems share the same understanding that for the soul to heal, one needs to use a "complete" Soul-Level Healing Process.

Chapter 9

SOUL-LEVEL HEALING AND THE SOUL-TRANSFORMATION PROCESS

In my previous book (*You're Not Going Crazy . . . You're Just Waking Up!*), it was explained how people regularly go through minor or major personal transformations, although often unbeknownst to them, and that these moments or periods of transformation have a purpose. One of the purposes for these transformational experiences is emptying our old, negative mental programs (core beliefs, issues, and patterns) and replacing them with new, positive programs—inspired by Spirit—involving love and self-worth or peace and healing. Other purposes for these moments of soul transformation are to encourage us to learn our lessons the easy way, rather than the hard way, and to begin experiencing the perks of living better lives.

Similar to the number of steps in the Soul-Level Healing Process, these life transformations explained in *You're Not Going Crazy . . . You're Just Waking*

Up! (referred to as the "Soul Transformation Process") occur in five stages: (1) Dismantling, (2) Emptiness, (3) Disorientation, (4) Rebuilding, and (5) A New Life.

Although these two processes are distinctly different, they are also similar and are, by no coincidence, directly related to one another. Both processes are concerned with healing, and each stage and step of the two processes are related, one to the other. To begin with, we *Recognize* that we are being (1) *Dismantled.* Then, we *Accept* that we feel (2) *Empty.* Next, we *Surrender* when we feel (3) *Disoriented.* Then, we *Refill,* or prepare to (4) *Rebuild.* Lastly, we *Give Thanks* for (5) *A New Life.*

There are two main differences between these two systems: The Soul-Level Healing Process deals with healing the core issues held within the soul—issues that cause most of our physical, emotional, relationship, and personal challenges. The Soul Transformation Process focuses on how and why our lives sometimes change or fall apart (become Dismantled) and how to walk through the naturally occurring 5-stages of transformation as gracefully as possible—using the opportunity to rise to the highest level of consciousness possible to begin creating A New Life.

Chapter 10

STEP I: RECOGNIZE

During the first step of the Soul-Level Healing Process, you make a choice to Recognize, or acknowledge, the issue at hand—the person or event that seems to be causing your negative experience. You Recognize that you are not happy with the situation as it is, and you are open to change. You no longer minimize, deny, or avoid the issue. Instead, you acknowledge the issue head on.

> *The power of decision is your one remaining*
> *freedom as a prisoner of this world. . . .*
> *As you decide so will you see.*
> **–ACIM** (Text 12, VII)

When you have reached the point of Recognizing your issue and are ready for a change, you have taken the first step in creating that change. Whether your issue at hand is major or minor and whether it involves finances or a relationship, health issues or something else, **the first step to changing the issue is the Recognition that there is an issue or problem.**

By Recognizing there is a problem, you are accomplishing the following essentials for Soul-Level Healing: (1) You are choosing a state of openness and humility—meaning you are like a blank canvas awaiting a new inspiration or creation. (2) You are acknowledging that what you had created or drawn to you previously (or are currently experiencing) is simply not working. (3) You are making a statement to God, yourself, and all energy in the universe that you are open to, and in need of, some assistance.

Reaching the level of Recognizing that you need a change may occur in one of two ways: the "easy way" or the "hard way." **As you move further along on your path of healing and spirituality, you less often will choose to learn your lessons the hard way** (through drama, hardship, and repetition of your challenging issues). The Recognition that you need a change may occur to you consciously or unconsciously. However, the more conscious you are of such decisions, the better assured you are of developing greater mindfulness and spiritual awareness through your healing process.

Recognizing that you need, and are ready for, a change can take many forms, or result from many challenges, that include any of the following:

- Loss (of job, partner, family member, etc.)
- An accident or perhaps even a near-death experience
- Depression or lack of passion for life
- Blocks to life-direction or inspiration
- Relationship challenges
- Any other experience that lacks the presence of Love, Peace, Joy, and Abundance

Whenever you take a vulnerable moment to honestly think or speak outwardly about a primary issue or problem in your life, it is a form of prayer. It may look different on the outside, but this form of prayer is just as valid as a prayer wherein a person stands or kneels down and says, "Dear God, I am in trouble and need some help with this illness (relationship, etc.)." Similar to this example of a person in prayer, when Recognizing a problem, you are acknowledging the issue at hand. The difference, however, is that you no longer are merely asking God to "fix the problem." Instead, you are (1) stating the problem as you see it; (2) stating that you are open to the idea that you may not understand the problem at its deepest level; (3) stating that you are moving into a deeper process of "Accepting" your part in creating this experience for the possible lessons to be learned; and (4) stating that you are ready to Refill your heart and soul with more love-based programs and patterns for A New Life.

CASE HISTORIES

The case histories chosen for these next few sections are the same cases, progressed from one step of the Soul-Level Healing Process to the next. Although the names have been changed, the case histories are authentic. These samples of cases are chosen for having fairly common subject matter—even if seeming somewhat unusual. We have purposely avoided using case histories that are too dramatic or tragic in their content.

CASE HISTORY #1: Janine

Issue: Had a session due to concerns with loneliness and a lack of dating.

Recognizing Statement: "I *Recognize* that I have not dated in 10 years."

CASE HISTORY #2: Andrea

Issue: Having health challenges wherein she was having difficulty breathing.

Recognizing Statement: "I *Recognize* that I am having difficulty breathing."

CASE HISTORY #3: Paul

Issue: Seemed incapable of committing to a relationship and suffered panic attacks whenever entering more serious stages of relationships.

Recognizing Statement: "I *Recognize* that I have panic attacks whenever I get close to a romantic partner."

CASE HISTORY #4: Arlene

Issue: A public speaker who was extremely overweight and had used all forms of diets but with no success.

Recognizing Statement: "I *Recognize* that I am over-weight and that this affects my health and self-image."

CASE HISTORY #5: Claire

Issue: Suffered most of her life from the physical and emotional effects of sexual abuse.

Recognizing Statement: "I *Recognize* that I have severe pain in my pelvic area and genitals when engaging in any form of sexual activity.

Chapter 11

STEP II: ACCEPT

The steps of Recognizing and Accepting are crucial to the healing process because most people go to great lengths to avoid dealing with their hurts and resentments. Most people choose to "fight, flight, or freeze." Others may choose to minimize or make excuses for their problems. Still others may choose the tactic of complaining or bemoaning their problems but never actually taking measures to make improvements. Whatever the case, only the most courageous people choose to practice Recognizing and then Accepting whatever is troubling them. Bravely confronting your issues face-to-face and walking through them (rather than running from your problems or going around them in an attempt to avoid them) helps to create true healing with lasting effects.

This step, important towards lasting healing, is not merely the passive "Accepting" of your situation as it is—certainly not in the sense of perceiving yourself as a "victim." On the contrary, in this step of the Soul-Level Healing Process, you primarily are Accepting any lessons or messages the problem or experience is presenting to you. Despite what you may think is going on in your life, there is far more occurring beneath the surface. As *A Course in Miracle*s so aptly asserts, "I am never upset for the reason I think." (Les. 5)

During this step in the Soul-Level Healing Process, you also Accept that there are some negative emotions behind the crisis or issue you are now experiencing and that there are deeper memories behind these emotions. In order to delve more deeply into the underlying cause of your issue, in the Acceptance Step, you can use a process referred to as "tracking." This term is chosen because you are "tracking down" the causes of your problem, much like *tracking* an animal by following its footprints. Tracking is similar to a form of "free association" that can help to identify some of the negative emotions behind your current issue/crisis. The tracking process includes asking yourself what emotions the person or event is bringing up in you and allowing three or four emotions to spontaneously come into your awareness. Such honest soul-searching often brings up old hurts—sometimes expected and sometimes unexpected—often accompanied by tears.

> *Nothing is hidden that will not be disclosed,*
> *nor is anything secret that will not become*
> *known and come to light.*
>
> **–The Bible,** Luke 8:17

Next, you identify the memories from your life wherein you had similar feelings and/or experiences. For example, if you Recognize that you are currently starting a "new" job, you may discover (during the tracking portion of the Acceptance Step) that starting a new job brings up anxiety, fear of the unknown, and self-esteem issues rooted in memories of the past. As you continue tracking these emotions, you may discover a memory of having these same feelings many years ago as a child when you were starting in a "new" school in a "new" town. The current experience is only serving to trigger old unhealed wounds, which will ultimately be Surrendered in a later part of the Soul-Level Healing Process.

Using the "tracking" process to uncover what lurks beneath the surface of what you think is the reason for your upset allows you to more accurately identify the "core issues" hidden behind what you once perceived as your primary issue or problem. Prior to tracking, you may have assumed that these strong, inner emotions were experienced simply because of your current outwardly manifested problem. After all, it is reasonable to assume, for example, that if your primary problem is losing your home or a loved one, you would feel sad, angry or afraid. In actuality, these emotions already existed within you—even if you were unaware of them. More shocking than this revelation is the fact that *those* very emotions (from your unhealed wounds) are *causing* your current issue.

These strong, negative emotions behind your current issue are seemingly "hidden" within because of an event or a string of events that remain—unhealed and un-forgiven—in your heart and soul. The current primary problem in your life is not actually *causing* these negative emotions; instead, the problem is appearing in your life *be-cause* of these unhealed emotions. Consequently, even if you were able to escape your current problem through the passage of time or through some "sleight-of-hand" human manipulation that seems to fix it (such as replacing a lost love with yet another relationship), your core emotions would manifest a similar event and usually in a more dramatic form.

Therefore, it is wiser to heal the inward core emotions (the cause), rather than attempting to deal exclusively with the outward manifestations (the effect). **Healing the cause at the Soul-Level, in turn, will create the miracle of unraveling the problem. Eliminating the inner cause will help prevent the outer problem from recurring.** In other words, when you get the message behind a hurtful or problematic event or relationship, the messenger (which can be people, problems, an illness, etc.) often disappears. This "disappearing" might take place literally or symbolically.

You will believe that you are part of where you think you are. That is because you surround yourself with the environment you want. And you want it to protect the image of yourself [which includes your body] *that you have made. The image is part of this environment. What you see while you believe you are in it is seen through the eyes of the image.*
–ACIM (Les. 35)

The shortest form of this Soul-Level Healing Process could be distilled into such a prayer as the following: "I *Recognize* I have a problem (naming it), and I also *Accept* that hidden behind this situation are my unhealed wounds and lessons (known and/or unknown). I now *Surrender* to God, both the problem and my unhealed wounds that I know lie beneath the surface of what I think I see. I now choose to *Refill* all the space left by the issues I just Surrendered, with all that God truly intends for me, including Love, Peace, Joy, and Abundance. I *Give Thanks* that this process is complete and is already bringing me miracles of healing. Thank you! Thank you! Thank you! And so it is!"

Although this example distills the entire Soul-Level Healing Process into a simple prayer, do not underestimate the power found within that prayer—especially if heartfelt. This is not the type of prayer that informs

God of a challenge you are experiencing and how you want it fixed. Instead, this prayer is a powerful process wherein you not only *Recognize* that there is a problem but also acknowledge that there are deeper issues hidden behind the apparent problem. Additionally, you are *Accepting* responsibility for having held onto the hurts that are feeding the current challenge. You are then taking the prayer to the next level of healing by choosing to *Surrender* all aspects of the issue to Spirit.

These steps empower you through humility—which is essential for receiving true healing in any form. In fact, the very lack of humility may have brought on your crisis (whether large or small). Having *Surrendered*, you now have emptied a great deal of negative energy, hurts, blocks, and old issues that are responsible in part for sabotaging your life. Now that you have "made room for God," the next portion of the prayer invites the Spirit of God (Love, Peace, Joy, and Abundance) into your life in order to *Refill* your heart and soul. Lastly, when these four steps are completed, there is nothing left but to *Give Thanks*.

It is during this step ("Acceptance") in the Soul-Level Healing Process that you choose either the short, medium, or long form of the healing process. (See Worksheets #1, #2, and #3 at the back of the book for a detailed description of the Soul-Level Healing Process in all three forms.)

In addition to using the short form of the healing process, exemplified in the above prayer, you also can use either the medium or the long form. These lengthier forms differ from the short form mainly in that some of the steps are experienced as a deeper, cathartic process. This purging is achieved through deeper introspection (the medium form) or, when necessary, through intensely cathartic releasing of emotions and hurts (the long form). In the latter case, there are specific techniques that may prove beneficial, such as those found in Alexander Lowen's "bioenergetics" or any other mode of "body-centered psychotherapy."

No matter which form of the healing process you choose (short, medium, or long), all have the potential to be equally effective. **To assume that the more intense form of the process is "better" would be to imply that emotional release has more power than prayerful release, and this is simply not the case.** The most effective form is the one that best fits the recipient, the particular situation, and the length of time available for doing the process. Furthermore, as people consistently use the long form and begin to heal, they usually discover they now need only the shorter form to create an instant shift in whatever challenge befalls them.

Whatever form of the process you choose, it is essential that you move through all five steps in order to experience a "complete" healing. In other words, it is essential that you experience a form of the healing process that involves thoroughly Emptying yourself of the past and Refilling with A New Life. These two phases of healing (Emptying and Refilling) are best done in the specific five steps to healing presented in this book. Your highest good is not served by using only one simple technique, such as "positive affirmations," and expecting a *complete* healing. Although this single technique might be helpful to some degree, especially when you need to do some Refilling, it most often will remain limited in its effectiveness when not used in conjunction with the other steps of the Soul-Level Healing Process.

CASE HISTORIES

CASE HISTORY #1: Janine

Accepting Statement: "I *Accept* that hidden behind not dating for 10 years are some negative emotions such as anger, sadness, and loneliness." [Moved into longer form of the healing process] "Also hidden behind not dating for 10 years and feeling sad, angry, and lonely are memories of my former husband who was gone all the time (leaving me at home) and turned out to be having an affair." [Began releasing deep tears of sadness]

CASE HISTORY #2: Andrea

Accepting Statement: "I *Accept* that hidden behind my difficulty breathing are some negative emotions such as fear, panic, anxiety, and feeling controlled or confined." [Moved into longer form of the healing process to see if any other events in her life felt similar] "Also hidden behind my panic attacks are memories my sister and I being little girls and both of us being very sick with lung problems. And I remember that we couldn't breathe and eventually my sister died. This made me feel very guilty for living. I felt like I took her air away from her." [potentially causing Andrea to now refuse to allow herself to breathe easily]

CASE HISTORY #3: Paul

Accepting Statement: "I *Accept* that hidden behind my panic attacks are also emotions such as fear, feeling pressured, and feeling not good enough." [Moved into longer form of the healing process] "Also hidden behind my panic attacks are memories of my alcoholic father who always seemed to destroy anything I loved and taught me that nothing I did was good enough."

CASE HISTORY #4: Arlene

Accepting Statement: "I *Accept* that hidden behind my being overweight are feelings of embarrassment, sadness, humiliation, and hurt." [Moved into longer form of the healing process] "Also hidden behind my being overweight are memories of being a little girl who enjoyed playing outside (but often got in severe trouble for getting my dresses dirty or torn while playing outside). Then one day, my dad took an old canvas, animal-feed bag and cut holes in it for my head, arms, and, legs and made me wear it as my new dress—even in front of our neighbors. I was ashamed and humiliated and I can see how the shape of that bag became my body and our neighbors became my audiences."

CASE HISTORY #5: Claire

Accepting Statement: "I *Accept* that hidden behind my physical pain and discomfort are negative emotions of pain and discomfort, as well as shame and anger due to my sexual abuse as a child." [Added anger release exercise, followed by Claire being physically held/cradled and gently rocked back and forth]

Chapter 12

STEP III: SURRENDER

At this point in the Soul-Level Healing Process, it is time to complete the releasing of any emotions (tears, rage, etc.) that surfaced during the previous step. Here you also take time to prayerfully Surrender *everything* that has come up thus far, which includes the original issue in step one, as well as the emotions and memories that arose in step two. Here you **visualize and feel the negative emotions and thoughts associated with the problem and the past causes all being removed from your mind, body, soul, and energy-systems.** They no longer can affect you, or attach to you, since they no longer are in alignment with who you are—or who you are about to become.

The step of Surrender can take one or more forms that include the following: prayerfully giving some negative emotion, thought, or issue to God; crying it away; releasing through deep sighing breaths; setting an intention to release; journaling or writing a goodbye note, then burning it, and seeing it dissipate as smoke into the ether.

During this step, you are Surrendering all of the people (including yourself), memories, events, emotions, and so forth to God. **The key to success is in Surrendering everything as completely and unconditionally as possible—thereby allowing yourself to become empty and open for being Refilled with the Loving Presence of God.**

> *Hold onto nothing. Do not bring with you one*
> *thought the past has taught, nor one belief you*
> *ever learned before from anything. . . . come*
> *with wholly empty hands unto your God.*
>
> **–ACIM** (Les. 189)

Ultimately, the Soul-Level Healing Process is not unlike gardening, with the Surrender Step being the time spent pulling out the rocks and weeds that would otherwise undermine your garden. This "weeding" and freeing-up of space, in turn, makes room for the seeds of A New Life to be "planted" in the Refilling Step.

CASE HISTORIES

CASE HISTORY #1: Janine

Surrendering Statement: "I *Surrender* Steven (my ex-husband), my negative emotions, and my lack of relationships to you God." [Added a goodbye ceremony for ex-husband]

CASE HISTORY #2: Andrea

Surrendering Statement: "I *Surrender* my body, my breath, my guilt, and most of all, my sister to you God." [Added a very tearful goodbye ceremony for sister]

CASE HISTORY #3: Paul

Surrendering Statement: "I *Surrender* my anxiety, my father, and the future of my relationships to you God."

CASE HISTORY #4: Arlene

Surrendering Statement: "I *Surrender* my body and my weight, as well as my dad, my neighbors, and all my memories to you God." [Added a visualization of Arlene seeing herself as a little girl removing the old, canvas sack she once wore and then peeling off her body to expose a being of light (her soul), beneath her skin]

CASE HISTORY #5: Claire

Surrendering Statement: "I *Surrender* my body, my pain, my sexuality, and my memories of abuse to you, God."

Chapter 13

STEP IV: REFILLING

The Refilling Step follows the emptying out that occurs during the steps of Recognizing, Accepting, and Surrendering. **Once you have emptied yourself of an issue from the past, you must then Refill your mind and soul with something new.** Although this need for Refilling may seem obvious, Refilling is the most neglected and overlooked step in nearly all forms of healing—especially emotional healing.

During the Refilling Step in the Soul-Level Healing Process, you can use any technique that effectively reprograms your mind, body, and soul with the concepts of A New Life. The techniques for Refilling most commonly used in the Soul-Level Healing Process are (1) mental concentration, (2) inspirational visualization, (3) inspired actions, (4) sharing with others, and (5) giving thanks.

MENTAL CONCENTRATION is the first tool used for Refilling. Initially, when you engage in mental concentration for Refilling in the Soul-Level Healing Process, you need to select a couple of focus words (commonly referred to as a mantra). These focus words should be synonymous with God and possibly the opposite of the negative feelings you previously may have been experiencing. For example, if you felt *attacked*, call in "safety;" if you felt *confused*, call in "clarity of thought;" if you felt *fear of being alone*, call in "God's Loving Embrace;" if you felt *anger*, call in "peace."

Whatever word or two you choose (for example, "Love and Self-Worth," "Peace and Healing," "Joy and Abundance," etc.), it is imperative that you understand that these words become much like your new name or identity. Furthermore, the origin, meaning, and spiritual vibration of your new name, or new focus, will become the foundation of your New Life. Spirit, by any name, now becomes your new "core belief," which will then replace your old core issues and patterns (and their manifestations) with an entirely new, positive set of programs.

Core beliefs are important because the world you see and experience is based not merely on your "thoughts," as so many teachings profess. Instead, **the world you see and experience is based on the foundation of your belief system** stored in your heart and soul—your higher mind. More specifically, your belief system is founded on, or arises from, the belief of what you are. **Who**

Energy pours in and fills the 3rd eye

The energy then flows down into the heart

The energy then spreads out and through the body

REFILLING THROUGH FOCUS

#1 Program your mind: As you inhale, draw in the Presence of God (in the form of light) through your head/mind and down into your heart, simultaneously repeating silently your 1-2 focus words (mantra).

#2 Program your heart and soul: While holding the energy in your heart-center for just 1-2 seconds, silently repeat your 1-2 words again, thus programming your heart and soul.

#3 Program every cell of the body: As you exhale, allow this new energy to wash over and cleanse all parts of your body, simultaneously repeating, "And so it is!"

NOTE: Repeat this process 1-2 dozen times and close by either Giving Thanks or by spending 5-10 minutes in "inspired visualization" and then Giving Thanks.

you believe you are (a holy being of Light or a limited and frail human being) then determines the nature of your thoughts, emotions, and experiences.

> *By establishing your Source, it establishes*
> *your Identity, and it then describes you as*
> *you must really be in truth.*
> **–ACIM** (Les. 35)

Since you are *not* really separate from God, it shouldn't be too complicated to connect with God's Consciousness. All you need do is start and end each day with the Love, Healing, and Guidance of God by calling Its Holy Presence into your heart and soul through the concentration exercise of Refilling. Also, be sure to reconnect by Refilling any time possible throughout the day—especially when needed. Again, connecting with God need not be a complicated concept or a lengthy technique. "One can easily give God only an instant, and in that instant join with Him completely." Just as easily, one can "sit still an hour with eyes closed and accomplish nothing." *–ACIM* (Manual 16, 4)

INSPIRATIONAL VISUALIZATION is the next tool for Refilling and involves imagining your mind and body being filled with a brilliant light—the Light of God. This light also comes from your angels, your spirit guides, and your soul family. This light heals you on every level—mind, body, and soul. Lastly, visualize yourself healed. See yourself looking, feeling, acting, and achieving that which you desire and deserve. Remember you are an extension of God, which means that **whatever you think upon and call into your life (as you Refill) is likely to manifest, particularly because you are now centered in your divinity and are using the power of your mind and soul as a co-creator.**

Whatever you want to be, start to develop that pattern now. You can instill any trend in your consciousness right now, provided you inject a strong thought in your mind; then your actions and whole being will obey that thought.
–Paramahansa Yogananda

Visualization in the Refilling step is far more than the typical, self-centered thoughts or ambition-based imaginings commonly used. The New Life you are visualizing and co-creating is originating from Source, rather than from the little, ego-self. To assure this, **it is important that what you choose to visualize is congruent with your spiritual mantra, or focus words, such as "Peace and Joy."** To do so creates a certainty that Spirit is the Power behind these final, seed-planting steps.

When concentrating and visualizing A New Life, be sure to include detailed visualizations of all major categories of your life, such as health, finances, relationships, family, and work. Also, forget everything you presently know about yourself. **Within your conscious awareness, you need only focus on and evoke Divine Presence. You then will enter a state of consciousness beyond time, turmoil, and needs—a state wherein you** *experience* **the answer to the prayer at the heart of your visualization.** This answer will then irresistibly rush into your life to manifest itself, like the most romantic of meetings.

Using the will does not necessitate physical or mental strain. Exertion of conscious will means a cool, calm, determined, increasingly steady and smooth—flowing effort of the attention and the whole being toward attaining a definite goal.

–Paramahansa Yogananda

INSPIRED ACTIONS are the third tool in the Refilling step. This involves seeing to it that all of your daily actions and decisions are congruent, or in alignment, with your "focus words" and the images of your visualizations. **If your focus words and visualization images are much like seeds being planted in your mind**

and soul, then your daily actions and decisions are like food and water for those seeds. Therefore, choose healthy food and water that will help your seeds grow and refuse the unhealthy actions and decisions that will destroy your new seeds.

When making decisions between various actions, the average person often feels torn between two or more options, which means being caught in the world of duality, or out of touch with God's Reality of perfect Oneness. Instead, when making a decision, you can use your focus words (or mantra) to separate the valuable from the invaluable—the necessary, or best, decision from the unnecessary, or "wrong," decision. Now, with the aid of your Refilling mantra, there is only ONE option, which is discovered by being in your ONE MIND—your right mind—the mind blessed by God. Now you choose only that which nurtures and feeds the seeds of your New Life—your focus word(s). As an expression of being focused, or single-minded, you accept no other option.

SHARING WITH OTHERS, the gifts or fruits of your new healing and awakening, is the fourth and final tool in Refilling. Failing to do so, may very well mean having the fruits of your transformation "die on the vine." The Love and Peace (or Truth) that you claim for yourself in the Refilling Step of your Soul-

Level Healing must be extended and shared as a means of anchoring them into your consciousness—permanently. As *A Course in Miracles* makes clear, "giving and receiving are the same." You can "receive" only that which you "give away." The Love and Peace you claim for yourself when Refilling are "a vision . . . which you must share with everyone you see, for otherwise you will behold it not." (*ACIM*, Text, p. 668)

GIVING THANKS is the fifth tool that is used to anchor in that which you have chosen as your new "reality," but this tool is covered in the next chapter as a step of its own.

CASE HISTORIES

CASE HISTORY #1: Janine

Refilling Statement: "I *Refill* my heart and soul, my mind, and my life with God's Love and Self-Worth." [Adding long form of the healing process] Visualization was done, specifically adding vivid pictures of what a healthy, reciprocal relationship would look like.

CASE HISTORY #2: Andrea

Refilling Statement: [Healing work was done on the torso to assist lungs and breathing] "I *Refill* with the Presence of God into every breath and allow myself to be filled with Love and Inspiration." [Also, the soul of her sister was visualized being drawn into her heart and soul, so the two of them would be spiritual sisters—giving each other life, breath and a healed relationship]

CASE HISTORY #3: Paul

Refilling Statement: "I *Refill* my soul and every part of my body with Peace and Joy."

CASE HISTORY #4: Arlene

Refilling Statement: "I *Refill* my body and soul with God's perfect Presence, as Love and Self-Worth."

CASE HISTORY #5: Claire

Refilling Statement: "I *Refill* my body—especially my pelvis—with Love, Peace, and Safety."

Chapter 14

STEP V: GIVE THANKS

This final step in the Soul-Level Healing Process, Giving Thanks or an expression of gratitude, is the best way to bring closure to all the releasing and Refilling that you accomplished while working on your issue.

Gratitude is one of the most important, yet underestimated, attitudes and tools for growth. **It is impossible to experience a true spiritual awakening without understanding and applying gratitude.** Giving Thanks tells the universe that you have completed the healing process related to the current issue and have released ALL the feelings and memories behind it. Also, Giving Thanks allows for blessings to come your way, because you now have more space "freed up" to fill yourself with Love, Peace, Joy, and Abundance—space that was once occupied by emptiness, fear, and low self-worth.

The free expression of gratitude is one of the surest signs that you have reached an empowering and vital level of consciousness—a state of Acceptance. One of the major steps towards Christ Consciousness, Acceptance, is primarily motivated by gratitude, or Giving Thanks. **To fully experience Acceptance, we need to embrace Gratitude as our dearest friend, whose name we speak often.** If we want to experience a greater abundance manifested as financial security, love, friendship, and a sense of God's Presence, we must first embrace and Accept our present state (or level)—which also means Accepting our part in creating our current situations.

An Accepting state of consciousness allows you to **Give Thanks for what you already have, prior to attempting to improve any given situation.** For example, practice Giving Thanks (feeling peace and Acceptance) for your body "as it is" *before* expecting a permanent change in that same body. Or, if you are on food stamps, Give Thanks for *that* form of prosperity *before* expecting a permanent increase in income. Or, practice loving the person or job you have (as much as possible) *before* leaving for another.

Giving Thanks brings closure to the past (and its lessons), as well as assists in the manifestation of A New Life (and its gifts). There is one precaution, however: Be careful not to Give Thanks with an attitude of self-pity. It is not in your best interest to say, "I am grateful for even the little I have" with an attitude of "woe is me" or even false humility. Instead, the Giving Thanks recommended in this final step of the Soul-Level Healing Process comes from a sense of worthiness, feels sincere and empowering, and brings a smile to your face.

When looking over your life as you heal at the level of heart and soul, you begin to feel a lightness in your heart when you contemplate all of the experiences you have had in life, including your past relationships. With a highly developed "attitude of gratitude," you truly multiply the love and joy you feel towards everyone you have ever known.

The same applies to all aspects of life. Be grateful to God, to yourself, and to everyone in your life—past, present, and future. Gratitude is proactive, rather than passive. **Gratitude demonstrates an attitude of love, rather than fear; Acceptance, rather than control and resistance; and appreciating, rather than taking for granted.** Gratitude in all its many forms results in a more joy-filled life. As feelings of gratitude increase, you begin to witness newly emerging experiences for which it is progressively easier to Give Thanks. An attitude of gratitude breeds more loving, nurturing relationships; a greater sense of prosperity and abundance; a healthier body; a greater sense of self-worth; and a more consistent connection to God.

This is not to say that challenges do not arise when we are grateful. Quite the contrary! We all experience challenges in our lives. However, as we heal and draw more of God into all aspects of ourselves, we will experience fewer challenges, and we will tend to move through challenges more quickly and with more ease. We also will lighten our loads and greatly alter the way we *perceive* such challenges. **As we nurture and develop Gratitude, we progress to a more expanded vision—trusting our divinity and continuing forward on our spiritual, healing paths.**

Finally, Gratitude is something to be expressed HERE AND NOW for what already is present. It is not a "thank you" to be applied only *after* we receive something we want or only for the things we perceive as "good." **Before we experience Heaven in its totality, we will first experience it here on earth.** The experiencing of Heaven on earth (the healing of the soul) is brought to fruition through gratitude for each and every aspect of our lives.

> *Give thanks for unknown blessings*
> *already on their way.*
>
> **—Native American Prayer**

CASE HISTORIES

CASE HISTORY #1: Janine

Giving Thanks Statement: "I *Give Thanks* to God for the Guidance to do this healing work and for Steven popping up during this work, as I know we needed closure. I also *Give Thanks* for the New Life that Love and Self-worth are already bringing to me. And so it is!"

Outcome: After 10 years without a single date, Janine began dating on a regular basis only three days after her Soul-Level Healing session.

CASE HISTORY #2: Andrea

Giving Thanks Statement: I *Give Thanks* for having gotten back my breath, my life, and my sister."

Outcome: After 35 years of having difficulty with breathing, Andrea's lungs felt open for the first time. She also felt an incredible emotional relief and several years later reports to have had no recurrence of her previous challenges.

CASE HISTORY #3: Paul

Giving Thanks Statement: "I *Give Thanks* for my healing and for the release of my father's effects on me. I also *Give Thanks* for the Peace and Joy that fill my heart and my life."

Outcome: Paul's panic attacks all but vanished immediately and were gone completely within a couple of months. Within 8-9 months, he entered his first serious relationship without ill effects and continued developing this relationship until he was married—happily now for 8 years.

CASE HISTORY #4: Arlene

Giving Thanks Statement: "I *Give Thanks* for my body and my new image of myself as a child. I also *Give Thanks* for the people and memories that arose during this healing session. I also *Give Thanks* for my new image of Love and Self-Worth."

Outcome: Within 6 months, Arlene was able to lose at least half of her excess weight, which positively affected her health and her success. More importantly, however, Arlene no longer felt the negative charge she once had for any weight she still retained.

CASE HISTORY #5: Claire

Giving Thanks Statement: "I *Give Thanks* for this healing of my pain and my past abuse. I also *Give Thanks* that I have received an opportunity to re-experience my sexuality from a state of innocence and healthiness."

Outcome: Six months later, when she returned for a follow-up session, Claire reported that during these last several months she experienced the first pain free sexual experience of her life, which has now lasted 3 years.

Chapter 15

SUMMARY AND CONCLUSION

The ultimate prerequisite for effective, permanent healing at the level of the soul (a miracle), is that God/Spirit remains our primary focus. God must remain the Alpha and Omega (first and final) priority in our lives and in every decision we make. Any other focus—especially a focus of a material nature—would be less than complete.

Day by day, day by day, oh dear Lord, three things I pray: To see Thee more clearly, love Thee more dearly, follow Thee more nearly, day by day.

–Robin Lamont & Co. (Song: "Day by Day")

Once you become accustomed to using the Soul-Level Healing Process as a normal way of living, your life will never be the same. You can easily take just one step (Accepting, for example) together with the "Tracking Process" to efficiently and effectively discover what is really going on beneath the surface of both your small and large issues. Or, rather than doing only the tracking process, you can do an entire "short form" (lasting less than a minute) of the healing process to completely transform an issue.

Whichever the choice, practicing this healing process (in part or entirely) not only will work wonders on its own but also can greatly increase the efficiency of standard talk therapy and the effectiveness of physical healing—especially when used in totality.

Although going through the process of a Soul-Level Healing usually manifests in ways that often seem miraculous, it may take time for such shifts to materialize. Until then, the challenge is to "Accept what is," while steadfastly upholding the Truth that never changes—**all that is God's (Love, Peace, Joy, and Abundance) also belongs to you. This is everyone's Divine birthright.**

> *In the Lord, you are Light.*
> *Live as children of Light.*
> **–The Bible, Ephesians 5:8**

How refreshing and empowering . . . to choose to be so close to God and, through Soul-Level Healing, to play a responsible part as co-creators in the universe and in our lives. This means living with complete sacred consciousness—as in Eden. Being close to God also means being far beyond living single elements of sacredness (such as sacred healing, sacred sexuality, sacred geometry, etc.) and instead understanding all things to be sacred.

> *Though we travel the world over to find*
> *the beautiful, we must carry it with us*
> *or we find it not.*
>
> **–Ralph Waldo Emerson**

To rediscover Eden, we must first consciously reconnect to, or remember, our souls and then eventually remember our true identity—as Spirit. And to reconnect with our souls, we must first heal the wounds that keep us apart *from* our souls. When we heal these wounds, the effects are immeasurable: Our partners become *soul*-mates; our jobs become our *souls'* purposes; parenting becomes *soul*-parenting; and healing becomes Soul-Level Healing.

Throughout this book, you may have assumed that all you were learning was a "technique" referred to as "Soul-Level Healing." However, the use of the word "soul" in "Soul-Level Healing" does not merely imply a deep and effective healing technique. Instead, the "soul" in "Soul-Level Healing" also stands for what happens when we heal the soul. In such moments of soul healing, we are brought back to a state of living from the sacred space within our hearts. We are no longer living as though we have been exiled from the sacred garden of our soul. Instead, our souls and our lives are healed, restored, and brought back to Eden— our original Heaven on earth.

WORKSHEET #1
Soul-Level Healing Process: Short Form

This is the short form of the Soul-Level Healing Process and is therefore as simple as a five-part prayer. Although the short form is the simplest form, it still covers all five steps of what it takes to achieve a Soul-Level Healing. When practiced from your heart, it will have deep and profound effects.

Repeat the following quietly to yourself or out loud:

RECOGNIZE: "I *Recognize* I am struggling with _____ (insert the issue of your concern)." This issue might be an illness, a challenge in a relationship, the inability to buy a new house, the loss of a job, etc.

ACCEPT: "I *Accept* that hidden behind this situation are my unhealed wounds and lessons (known and/or unknown)."

SURRENDER: "I *Surrender* to God both the problem and my unhealed wounds that I know lie beneath the surface of what I think I see."

REFILL: "I *Refill* all the space left by the issues I just Surrendered with all that God truly intends for me, including Love, Peace, Joy, and Abundance."

GIVE THANKS: "I *Give Thanks* that this process is complete and is already bringing me miracles of healing. Thank you! Thank you! Thank you! And so it is!"

WORKSHEET #2
Soul-Level Healing Process: Medium Form

This is the medium form of the Soul-Level Healing Process, which takes you deeper into the underlying issues manifesting as your current challenge, as well as providing a deeper sense of Refilling with A New Life. Again, the most dramatic differences among the short, medium, and long forms of the Soul-Level Healing Process are mainly in the Acceptance and Refilling steps. In the Acceptance step you now delve far deeper into the hidden causes behind whatever you have brought up for healing. In the Refilling step you add a concentration exercise used to reprogram the heart with positive new thoughts.

Repeat the following quietly to yourself or out loud: RECOGNIZE: "I *Recognize* that I am struggling with_____ (insert the issue of your concern)." This issue might be an illness, a challenge in a relationship, the inability to buy a new house, the loss of a job, etc.

ACCEPT: "I *Accept* that hidden behind this situation are some negative emotions, such as _____, _____, and _____ (name approximately three negative emotions associated with the issue at hand, such as anger, sadness, frustration, betrayal, tiredness, etc.)." Now allow yourself to freely look back over your life to see if there are any other times when a person or event caused you to feel, most or all of, these same negative emotions. Once you recall an event—if one or more come to mind—make note of who or what it is, as you will be Surrendering it in the next step.

SURRENDER: "I *Surrender* my current crisis, all related people and past events, as well as all the related causes—known or unknown—to you, my Father/Mother God." Then, spend a moment feeling and visualizing the old burdens and wounds being lifted out of you and up into the sky, into the Light of God. Also, use your breath to viscerally release the old wounds on the next few exhalations.

REFILL: "I *Refill* all the space left by the issues I just Surrendered with all that God truly intends for me, including Love, Peace, Joy, and Abundance." Then, as you inhale deeply, imagine drawing light down into your heart-center from the heavens (symbolizing God). Simultaneously, concentrate on words such as "Love and Self-Worth" (or any other word or words, such as "Peace," "Joy," "Abundance," "Wholeness," etc., that most depict the God-like state of consciousness you desire). In so doing, you are programming your heart and soul with these new patterns. After anchoring these qualities (via words and feelings) into your heart-center, exhale slowly as you visualize the light spreading from your heart-center to every cell of your body, bathing you completely. As you do this, allow yourself to hear the words "And so it is." Then repeat this process approximately one to two dozen times.

GIVE THANKS: "I *Give Thanks* for this healing miracle. I *Give Thanks* for all the people and past events that arose during this session. I also *Give Thanks* for all the people and events that I chose to release, as well as to the New Life that I've taken time to visualize. The universe is already beginning to manifest these changes in my life. And so it is!"

WORKSHEET #3
Soul-Level Healing Process: Long Form

This is the long form of the Soul-Level Healing Process, which takes you even deeper into the underlying issues manifesting as your current challenge, as well as providing a deeper sense of Refilling with A New Life. Again, the differences between the medium and the long forms are found in the Acceptance and Refilling steps. In the Acceptance step you delve even deeper into the soul to find the hidden causes behind whatever you have brought up for healing. At this point, you might then add some form of cathartic process to aid in releasing whatever has come up for healing. In the Refilling step, you now add (to the concentration exercise found in the medium form) a visualization exercise used to reprogram the mind, heart, and soul with positive new beliefs and programs.

Repeat the following quietly to yourself or out loud:
RECOGNIZE: "I *Recognize* I am struggling with _____ (insert the issue of your concern)." This issue might be an illness, a challenge in a relationship, the inability to buy a new house, the loss of a job, etc.
ACCEPT: "I *Accept* that hidden behind this situation are some negative emotions, such as _____, _____, and _____ (name approximate-

ly three negative emotions associated with the issue at hand, such as anger, sadness, frustration, betrayal, tiredness, etc.)." Now allow yourself to freely look back over your life to see if there are any other times when a person or event caused you to feel, most or all of, these same negative emotions. After one or more events or persons come to mind, note who or what they are because you will be Surrendering them all in the next step.

Next, you can add some form of cathartic release, such as an anger release exercise, an imagined dialog with previous "offenders," a goodbye exercise (as found in the book appendix) for anyone with whom you need closure—including those who have passed away.

SURRENDER: "I *Surrender* my current crisis, all related people and past events, as well as all the related causes—known or unknown—to you, my Father/Mother God." Then, spend a moment feeling and visualizing the old burdens and wounds being lifted out of you and up into the sky, into the Light of God. Also, use your breath to viscerally release the old wounds on the next few exhalations.

REFILL: "I *Refill* all the space left by the issues I just Surrendered with all that God truly intends for me, including Love, Peace, Joy, and Abundance." Then, as you inhale deeply, imagine drawing light down into your heart-center from the heavens (symbolizing God). Simultaneously, concentrate on such words as "Love and Self-Worth" (or any other such word or words as "Peace," "Joy," "Abundance," "Wholeness," etc., that most depict the God-like state of consciousness you desire). In so doing, you are programming your heart and soul with these new patterns. After anchoring these qualities (via words and feelings) into your heart-center, exhale slowly as you visualize the light spreading from your heart-center to every cell of your body, bathing you completely. As you do this, allow yourself to hear the words "And so it is." Then repeat this process approximately one to two dozen times.

Next, spend at least 5-10 minutes visualizing and feeling your life as you would like it to be. Look at each major aspect of your life (such as health, finances, relationships, and work). Ask yourself, "If I am indeed filled with 'love and self-worth' (or whatever words you've chosen), what would my life look and feel like (in each of these major categories)?" Respond by visualizing and feeling the answer in a living form, as though it is already happening—right now. For example, if you were to choose to see yourself healthy, you might visualize and feel yourself exercising in a form that you enjoy (perhaps yoga). See yourself doing the yoga postures and feeling the effects in your body. This might include seeing and feeling your joints being more open and your body less stiff or sore.

GIVE THANKS: "I *Give Thanks* for this healing miracle. I Give Thanks for all the people and past events that arose during this session. I also Give Thanks for all the people and events that I chose to release, as well as to the New Life that I've taken time to visualize. The universe is already beginning to manifest these changes in my life. And so it is!"

Note: There is one last step in the long form of this exercise. It involves making sure that from now on your actions and decisions are, as often as possible, in alignment with your focus words and the New Life you have spent time visualizing. This means that every decision, action, and word that you choose needs to bring you closer to the new consciousness you desire and for which you are praying. Your actions and decisions should add to, rather than subtract from, the nurturing of Love, Peace, Joy, and Abundance. They need to water and feed the seeds of your New Life that were planted in the Refilling step.

If your words and actions contribute to your long-term peace and happiness, they probably are the "right" decisions for you. If such actions and decisions conflict with your long-term wellbeing, they're probably not the best choices for you. In order to continue building your New Life and a new, healthier self with healthier boundaries, surrender your every thought, word, and action to a Power beyond the laws and logic of this world. If you follow the tangible guidance in your heart that clearly promotes love, rest assured that this guidance is inspiration, or the Voice of God.

APPENDIX A
Miscellaneous Healing Exercises

The following exercises can prove to be very effective if done individually but are best done as merely a part of one of the steps of a complete five stage, Soul-Level Healing Process.

Tracking Exercise
(Use in Step #2: Accept)

Tracking is an incredibly quick (yet powerful and effective) way to access the deeper issues behind nearly any issue, problem, illness, or crises. Anyone can learn to do tracking in a matter of minutes but greater skills can be nurtured to enhance its effects. These skills include one's healing or counseling skills but also one's intuitive skills, which are an invaluable asset to any form of healing or healing work.

1. Repeat the following quietly to yourself or out loud, "I *Recognize* I am struggling with _____ (insert the issue of your concern)." This issue might be an illness, a challenge in a relationship, the inability to buy a new house, the loss of a job, etc.

2. Then repeat, "I *Accept* that hidden behind this situation are some negative emotions, such as _____, _____, and _____ (name approximately

three negative emotions associated with the issue at hand, such as anger, sadness, frustration, betrayal, tiredness, etc.)."

3. Then repeat, "I also *Accept* that there are other times in my life when I similarly have felt this way, such as _____ (spontaneously fill in the blank with the most dominant memory of a person or incident in your life that similarly caused you to feel, most or all of, these same negative emotions)." Chances are, you have now "tracked down" something that was never healed to "completion" and is adding to or causing your current emotional crisis.

4. Once you Accept this, the issue is now uncovered, and you can choose to do some deeper cathartic work to assist in releasing the memories and/or energy around these emotions and memories. Ideally, this would all be followed by some prayerful form of *Surrender* and *Refilling* with images and actions that depict A New Life and then *Give Thanks*.

Anger Release Exercise
(Use in Step #2: Accept)

Throughout the healing process, whenever any old issues are dredged up, there may be a need to use a healthy means of processing the surfacing emotions—

especially anger. Some of the most common techniques for accessing and releasing anger are as follows:

1. **Hitting a Cushion or Mattress:** Some people who choose this option use tools, such as a tennis racket, while others just use their hands or fists. Whichever you choose, the idea is to slam your hands down onto the bed (or cushion), while exhaling or stating a word (or words) of frustration, such as "No!" or "I'm so angry!" over and over again, until you have exhausted most of your strength. This is a great way to override your conscious attempts to control your anger and keep it trapped inside.

2. **Kicking and Screaming:** While facing down on a bed or thick mat, begin kicking your legs (from the knee down) at a rapid pace. Also, you may choose to hammer your hands down onto the bed or mat. Every few seconds, you may choose to shout the same words mentioned above onto the bed or a pillow. Again, do this until you are nearly exhausted. Once you feel the releasing is complete, be sure to allow sufficient time to remain quiet and *feel* whatever is happening inside. You may feel some emotions percolating up and possibly the release of tears. Shortly after these emotions subside, always be sure to end with at least a minute or two of Refilling with God's Presence, followed by Giving Thanks.

Goodbye Ceremony/Exercise
(Use in Step #3: Surrender)

The purpose of the "Goodbye Exercise" varies from person to person. Some people need to say goodbye to a long lost friend, others to a deceased loved one, and still others, to someone who has behaved hurtfully.

There are different healing traditions that have some form of goodbye ceremony. In shamanism, for example, there are ways of cutting old ties. Other traditions utilize what is referred to as "cord cutting" when it comes to releasing the energetic ties that keep someone bound to us (or us to them) when in fact it is not for our highest good.

So, even though it can be a very painful decision and process, we all need to say goodbye to someone at some point in our lives. The difference is that we are not referring to a verbal goodbye and wave to someone we can see. Instead, it means saying goodbye to someone with whom we have energetic connections, which is best done in an empowering ceremony. This ceremony should be heart-felt and not necessarily be repeated verbatim.

Begin by imagining (in the room with you) an image of the person to whom you need to say goodbye. Then repeat the following:

1. "I am calling you _____ (insert name) into this

room so I can share my feelings about our life and relationship."

2. "My relationship with you has affected my life. It has affected my _____ (name whatever areas of your life you feel have been affected, such as health, tension level, nervous system, finances, confidence, relationships, parenting, etc.)."

3. "My relationship with you confused me (name possible ways in which this relationship might have confused you, such as making you feel unloved or unlovable, leaving you without closure, etc.)."

4. "My relationship with you scared me (name possible ways in which this relationship might have scared you, such as the person's anger causing you to feel frightened, abuses that might have scared you, unpredictable behaviors, etc.)."

5. "My relationship with you made me sad (name possible ways in which this relationship might have made you sad, such as the sadness arising from its ending, the person being gone, or the feeling that the relationship didn't have to turn out the way it did, etc.)."

6. "My relationship with you also made me feel hurt and angry (name possible ways in which this relationship might have made you feel hurt and angry,

such as through neglectful behaviors, physical abuses, selfishness, betrayal, etc.)."

7. "Again, our relationship has affected my life and it's time to let go of the effects of our relationship. And to do that, I have to let you go. Today I am letting you go to a whole new level of completion."

8. Now begin to watch the person's image fade away over the next 30-60 seconds, as you repeat saying "Goodbye" to them three times, with 10-15 seconds between each repetition. Each time you say "Goodbye," visualize the person fading more and more. After the first repetition of "Goodbye," tell the person, "I am releasing you unconditionally and for all time." After the second repetition, tell the person, "With you go all vows, debts, karma, agreements, and contracts between us." After the third repetition, tell the person, "Even at the risk of your disappointment or disapproval (if this applies), I have to let you go." The final repetition also means an acceptance of this person's failure to be or to do something you wanted him or her to be or to do (for example, to live longer, to "see" you, to be there for you, etc.). Vividly see the person's image fading completely way.

9. Now take a moment to "feel" (a general feeling only, not a detailed visualization) what your life would

have been like if you had not had to endure some of these hurtful losses or circumstance. Imagine how you might have been different (again, not in detail, but would you be a happier person, healthier, more relaxed, etc.).

10. Lastly, just as you began this ceremony by speaking to the person's human, limited personality, you now repeat the following to the person's soul: "I know that you are out there somewhere and can hear me. So I choose to now share with you that I know and affirm that in you there is a spark of God's Light. This spark cannot die, be sick, be hurt or hurtful, or be addicted. This spark is the part of you made in God's image, and it is the part of you I wish I would have known. And although I might sometimes feel sadness that we may have missed knowing this better part of each other, I am grateful to see/feel it now."

Close the ceremony by possibly seeing the person as a being of light. Then release him or her into the universe as you repeat, "I release you to be everything you are truly meant to be. And, in releasing you, I am also releasing myself." If you loved the person and were close to him or her, you can close the visualization by seeing the person turn into a soft mist of colorful light, and then draw his or her soul/essence into your own heart and soul through your breath. Repeat (a few times) this visualization of merging with the person. Then close by Giving Thanks for sharing this wonderful healing ceremony and for the permanent affects it will have in your life—beginning now!

Refilling Exercise
(Use in Step #4: Refill)

The following is perhaps the most effective exercise to assist the Refilling step. This exercise is similar to what many shamans refer to as "dreaming the world into being." The best time to practice is each morning and evening, when you first wake up and before going to sleep, as follows:

While inhaling deeply, imagine drawing light through the top of your head from the heavens (symbolizing God). On that in-breath, allow this energy to be drawn down into your heart-center, as you simultaneously concentrate on the words "love and self-worth" (or any other word or words you choose as your focus words (or mantra), such as "Peace," "Joy," "Abundance," "Wholeness," etc. These words need to depict the new state of consciousness you desire. In so doing, you are programming your heart and soul with these new patterns. After anchoring these qualities (through words and feelings) into your heart-center, exhale slowly as you allow the light to spread from your heart-center to every cell in your body, bathing you completely. As you do this, allow yourself to hear the words "And so it is." Then Repeat this process approximately one or two dozen times before proceeding to step two. Again, as your draw the energy and vibration of your chosen focus words through your head, you are programming your mind with their meaning. When the energy enters your heart, you are reprogramming your heart and soul. Lastly, when you exhale and allow the energy to pass through your body, you are reprogramming the very cells of your body. Just this step alone, allows every aspect of your being to be reprogrammed with a new level of Spiritual Presence.

Spend at least 5-10 minutes visualizing and feeling your life as you would like it to be. Look at each major aspect of your life (such as health, finances, relationships, and work). Ask yourself, "If I am indeed filled with 'love and self-worth' (or whatever words you've chosen), what would my life look and feel like (in each major category)?" Respond by visualizing and feeling the answer in a living form, as though it is already happening—right now. For example, if you were to choose to see yourself healthy, you might visualize and feel yourself exercising in a form that you enjoy (perhaps yoga). See yourself doing the yoga postures and feeling the effects in your body. This might include seeing and feeling your joints being more open and your body less stiff or sore.

Always close such exercises by Giving Thanks in advance that anything you just imagined, while attuned to Spirit and aligned with your highest good, is already being brought into manifestation.

In addition to the aforementioned steps, be sure that every decision, action, and word that you choose from now on builds the New Life of love and self-worth for which you are praying. Your actions and decisions should add to, rather than subtract from, the nurturing of Love, Peace, Joy, and Abundance. If your words and actions contribute to your long-term peace and happiness, they probably are the "right" decisions for you. If such actions and decisions conflict with your long-term wellbeing, they're probably not the best choices for you. In order to continue building your New Life and a new, healthier self with healthier boundaries; surrender your every thought, word, and action to a Power beyond the laws and logic of this world. If you follow the tangible guidance in your heart that clearly promotes love, rest assured that this guidance is inspiration, or the Voice of God.

APPENDIX B
Testimonials for the Soul-Level Healing Process

As many times as I have heard people say, "Just Surrender" or "Just let it go" I have never really understood what that meant . . . until now. During my Soul-Level Healing Process, I was shown first-hand what it meant to feel my old wounds being lifted up and Surrendered to Spirit. I learned that this cannot be a quick nor intellectual process, but rather is a process of sincerity and humbleness.

–Jessica, WA

As part of what I learned in the Refilling step of the Soul-Level Healing Process, I am finally dating someone again. It had been way too long. My new partner is loving and attentive, which are both my focus words that I use to describe my life.

–Monique, Vancouver, Canada

I knew I had a few external issues and went to see Michael because I heard he could help me work on them. But when I was shown how to Accept the deeper internal issues that were causing my external issues, I was blown away. I have never felt that level of personal pain and I was shown that the pain was already there, already sitting inside of me, destroying my life. I had suppressed it for so many years, mainly because it was about my memories about being molested as a child. Michael was right there with me, guiding me and knowing (even before I knew) exactly when the next surge of tears or body convulsions would be coming. When it was over, Michael held me and gently caressed my head, the way a loving parent would treat a child if they had been hurt and neither of my parents had done this for me. When the session was over, Michael reminded me that it was now up to me to treat myself with the same gentleness that he had.

–Diane, NV

I recently had a Soul-Level Healing Session due to my ongoing panic attacks. Then, on the eve of my session another panic was beginning, so I just tried to relax but couldn't. I began breathing heavier and harder and I began to prepare myself for the terror I've been experiencing for years. I must have fallen asleep then, because I woke-up later and took a deep breath thinking I was going to feel fear, but there was none. The breath filled my solar plexus and there was room for lots more air. I just laid there experiencing my breath and I realized for years when I would inhale deeply there was a fear at the top of my breath, this is totally gone! I wept quietly for a long time, filling myself with breath, the beautiful light, joy and abundance.

–Pamela, CA

I can't imagine there is an easier way to heal. I made great progress just by honestly Recognizing my issues. I forgot what it meant to be courageous and having taken a look at what was really going on in my life has made me feel brave in ways I couldn't imagine. Now I use the technique of Recognizing my issues whenever I stray off center. I learned that the sooner I catch myself, the sooner I can get back on track.

–Brent, PA

Thank you for the healing session yesterday. After watching this beautiful sunset I went home and slept for 10 hours—something I have not done in many years. I loved the Refilling exercise. I actually shared it with a few of my children at school today who had some pain in their body. Thank you for sharing Gods light with us all and for being real. This teaches me to be more of who I am.

–Helen, Maui

After my Soul-Level Healing Session, and learning to Refill my soul, I feel like a totally different person; the fear is gone and it is really a new place for me to be. I have had several instances that I would have had much fear and there was absolutely none. Instead, I felt strong and confident. It is so awesome! I find myself crying with such gratitude and love that I don't have to carry that with me anymore. I can actually breathe and know that I am breathing . . . I can feel my heartbeat . . . There is no more pain at all . . . No more pain!!! Thank you God! The great thing is that when I told my husband about the session, he listened with tears in his eyes and he couldn't wait to hear more. We are anxious to begin our new relationship, using your suggestions, and I just know in my heart that I am going to be able to finally be present! Lastly, the Refilling exercise has already been having an effect on me. I am also actually beginning to feel sensations in my lower body . . . it is so exciting since I have not inhabited that part of my body in many, many years! It feels fabulous!

–Ginger, NY

I so VERY much appreciate the Soul-Level Healing Session I had recently. I am doing the Refilling exercises every morning and night, as well as throughout the day. I find they help me to get centered. Your healing energy is astonishing and I have felt it even after our session, at times, strongly and intensely. This is such a wonderful and precious gift to me! I am VERY impressed with your healing abilities and loving energy. You are a TRUE HEALER!

–Wendy, CA

My partner and I had a Soul-Level Healing Session, for which you graciously refused payment, as our home was in foreclosure. We wanted to let you know the "miracle" that occurred as a result. One of my friends has now agreed to finance our new home for us at 3% interest, and we're moving within a couple of weeks. Blessings to you always for helping us so much when we were in dire need. Thank you eternally for your part in the great "work."

–Patricia, MI

After my Soul-Level Healing Session, I woke up the next morning feeling physically lighter, like I lost 10 pounds, very cool. My abdomen was open, like the blanket that was on it, was lifted, no sensation of fear in that area. My shoulder which was worked on, feels tender, yet amazingly better. My knee was also worked on and I've had no discomfort going up and down the stairs. If I had to describe in one word what I felt like when I got out of bed, it would be ALIVE! Okay a second word: GRATEFUL!!!

–Terry, CT

I was totally floored by my Soul-Level Healing Session. For the rest of the day whenever I closed my eyes, my third eye was emblazoned with golden light. My back was no longer in pain; I felt a great sense of peace, and could not tell if my feet were touching the ground. Our session certainly surpassed all of my expectations.

–Nancy, MA

EXPLORING
SACRED SEXUALITY

Facilitated by Michael Mirdad, this workshop is a five-day intensive that synthesizes the most effective arts of sacred sexuality, including Tantra and Taoist sexology. This workshop also incorporates modern techniques of sexual healing. The event is for everyone, whether you are single, have a partner, are sexually active or not. In the safest and most sacred atmosphere, you will learn to develop and channel your own sexual energy to enhance health, vitality, and self awareness.

THE WORKSHOP ALSO FEATURES:

- Exercises for health, vitality, and rejuvenation
- Techniques for enhancing the intimacy in your relationships
- Self-awareness to heal sexual guilt, shame, and inhibitions
- An introduction to sexual anatomy and terminology
- Tantric and Taoist techniques to enhance your sexual experience
- Techniques for channeling your sexual energy into creative ecstasy

To apply for this workshop, please contact us at:
Grail Productions, PO Box 2783, Bellingham, WA 98227
360-671-8349 or office@grailproductions.com.

WORKSHOP INTENSIVES
Offered by Michael Mirdad

There are three primary workshop intensives offered by Michael Mirdad. The first, in the spring, is Healing: Body and Soul and is designed to bring the attendees to new levels of physical, emotional, and spiritual health, while also teaching them how to become healers (or better healers). The second, in the summer, is Living Mastery. This workshop is great for anyone who is ready to discover new levels of direction, responsibility, balance, and wholeness. The third workshop, in the fall, Initiations Into Christ Consciousness, teaches attendees to connect with their True (Christ) Self and deeper levels of spiritual awareness.

HEALING: BODY & SOUL

This workshop is a 5-day intensive for anyone seeking to receive physical and/or emotional healing or choosing to develop greater healing abilities. It is perfect for those wanting to renew their commitment to maintaining physical/emotional health and spiritual connectedness and includes training in herbology, massage, energy work, Tai Chi, acupressure, Reiki, emotional healing, yoga, cranial release, health intuitiveness.

"I am so grateful that the workshop re-ignited or deepened the healer in me. I absolutely loved using a combination of breath work, physical body work, intuition, and advanced techniques to trigger issues on a cellular level to bring them forth to be healed. We learned healing and counseling skills that most counselors don't even know!" –Ron, ONT

www.GrailProductions.com

159

LIVING MASTERY INTENSIVE

This workshop is a 5-day intensive for those who are prepared to live a life of fulfillment. It teaches how to experience the best life possible in every aspect of living. No other single event offers so much! Living Mastery is an advanced training for students and teachers of spirituality who are ready to learn how to manifest a spiritual, integrated, balanced, and prosperous life, as well as learning how to bring God and all spiritual learning into their daily lives and activities. Topics include the following: physical mastery–manifesting prosperity, living healthy through yoga and diet, and training in several healing arts; emotional mastery–developing psychic abilities, creating fulfilling relationships, and learning advanced emotional healing techniques; mental mastery–developing greater focus, learning effective meditation, and discovering your soul's purpose; and spiritual mastery–developing a life plan, learning true forgiveness, awakening higher levels of consciousness, and opening your heart center.

"I am so honored to have had the opportunity to experience five of the most amazing days of my life, while attending the Mastery Workshop. I became aware of my strength and endurance through rock climbing, yoga, and the obstacle course. I embraced exercises in past life regression and emotional healing. I was challenged doing exercises in cloud busting and learning the importance of focusing, as well as dividing and conquering life's obstacles. And I learned the importance of prayer and meditation and letting God live through me every instant of my life." –Janet, NY

INITIATIONS INTO
CHRIST CONSCIOUSNESS

This workshop is an advanced training for students and teachers of Christ Consciousness. It covers advanced teachings and spiritual concepts, as well as profound levels of application. Attendees learn to clear their centers of consciousness and live a life that reflects their higher self in mind, body, and soul. This workshop also covers the following: initiations into Christ Consciousness through rarely understood mystery teachings of Jesus–some of which were transferred to Mary Magdalene, clearing of various energy centers (chakras), the secret teachings of Christ, Jesus' missing years amongst the Essenes and the Mystery Temples, and experiencing your own spiritual baptism.

"There were so many wonderful activities at this workshop. The information about the history of the universe was clear, informative and intriguing. The closing initiation into the Christ Consciousness was transformative. When I lay down in the middle of the circle, I felt the amplification of energy, all the light, in my body. As my heart chakra opened, I felt as if my entire chest were being pulled up to the ceiling, while my breath was deep and being pulled through my body to my feet. I felt like I was in the zone of Jesus, Mary, and of course fellow attendees. I feel as though I have attained a new spiritual level." –Jean, OR

www.GrailProductions.com

SACRED SITES JOURNEYS

With Michael Mirdad

THE INITIATORY JOURNEY

Since the beginning of time, students and masters on the spiritual path have taken journeys of initiation to sacred sites. These holy places included France, Egypt, Central America, and Britain. Initiates brought with them a sacred technology to build temples, megaliths, and ascension sites for healing and for harnessing the Earth's grid system.

Today these journeys still serve as a powerful ritual for personal power and spiritual awakening for planet Earth and all its inhabitants. Come and join us in this personal and planetary awakening.

SAMPLES OF SOME OF OUR JOURNEYS

FRANCE
Grotto-Home of Mary Magdalene
St. Marie de La Mer
Lourdes
Sacred Cathar & Templar Sites
France's Mount of St. Michael

IRELAND
Newgrange
Sacred Hill of Tara
Numerous Ancient Goddess Sites

SCOTLAND
Findhorn
Scottish Highlands
Magical Iona Island
Rosslyn Chapel

ENGLAND
Crop Circles
Avebury & Stonehenge
Glastonbury Abbey
The Chalice Well
Numerous Arthurian Sites

GREECE
Delphi
Legendary Islands
Athens

EGYPT
Great Pyramids
Valley of the Kings
Karnak
Temples of the Nile

Price includes: international travel from US and back, shared lodging, tour guides, most meals, entrance to sacred sites, teaching sessions, and more. Space is limited! Contact us now to register or to get on our mailing list.

Grail Productions, PO Box 2783, Bellingham, WA 98227
For information: 360-671-8349 or office@grailproductions.com
Visit us at www.GrailProductions.com

ORDER FORM

To order any of our books or request more information on any of these publications, please copy and mail in this order form. You can also call our office or visit our website (see below) for a complete list of books, CDs, and DVDs.

Name_____

Address_____

City, State, Zip_____

Phone_____

Email_____

Please include any special instructions when ordering. Make checks payable to: Grail Productions.

_____

An Introduction to Tantra and Sacred Sexuality
_____ copies at $15.00 each =   _____

Sacred Sexuality: A Manual for Living Bliss
_____ copies at $25.00 each =   _____

Seven Initiations of the Spiritual Path
_____ copies at $15.00 each =   _____

You're Not Going Crazy...You're Just Waking Up!
_____ copies at $15.00 each =   _____

Healing the Heart & Soul
_____ copies at $15.00 each =   _____

Add $2.50 for S&H per book   _____

Total   _____

Grail Productions, PO Box 2783, Bellingham, WA 98227
For information: (360) 671-8349 or office@grailproductions.com
Visit us at www.GrailProductions.com

ABOUT THE AUTHOR

Michael Mirdad is a world-renowned spiritual teacher, healer, and author. He has worked as a healer and counselor for 30 years and is the author of the best-selling books, *The Seven Initiations of the Spiritual Path*, *An Introduction to Tantra and Sacred Sexuality*, and *You're Not Going Crazy . . . You're Just Waking Up!* Michael has facilitated thousands of classes, lectures, and workshops throughout the world on Mastery, Spirituality, Relationships, and Healing and is commonly referred to as a "teacher's teacher" and a "healer's healer." He has been featured as a keynote speaker in the world's largest expos and conferences, and has been on radio, television, and various internet programs. His work has been published in several leading magazines, including *Whole Self Times*, *Sedona Journal*, and *Yoga Journal*, as well as the cover feature in *Evolve* magazine. Michael Mirdad is respected as one of the finest and most diverse healers of our time and well-known for his ability to share the deepest teachings in a clear, applicable manner.